The Missing Cub

Chicago Cubs

DARCY FAST

with Jonathan Kravetz

PRESS

"Darcy Fast was a 6-foot 3inch, left handed-pitcher who shot through the Cubs minor league system. He made it to Chicago midway through his second professional season. Tell me a better name for a pitcher, Bill Hands? Rollie Fingers? Jack Armstrong? Bob Walk. Give me Darcy Rae Fast anytime."

Mike Murphy—
In Select Cubs Remain Memorable Footnotes

"I have known Darcy Fast personally for three years. He is a man of integrity, strength, and is an inspiration to us all. He has fulfilled every young boy's dream, and yet he has ultimately followed a more divine plan: God's plan. His journey is universal to all men.

Lyle Overbay, First Baseman—Toronto Blue Jays

"*The Missing Cub is a must read blend of Cubs history and the path a man can take through life to find his purpose.*"

Clayton Walker, Writer

"*I shared with Darcy those exciting but mostly agonizing days with the Cubs in the Leo Durocher era. We chased our dreams of the Major Leagues, but mostly we were faced with the politics and power-wielding specter of "Leo Durocher" in Chicago. He caused most of us to question our dream of the Major Leagues. I know I did. He made it tough on young guys. I was lucky, I was traded and I pursued my baseball dreams. Darcy was insightful (maybe with Leo's help) and he was shown his life's calling. I remember him as a teammate and thought we would win the World Series together.*"

Jim Colborn, Pitching Coach — Pittsburgh Pirates

Nolan Ryan's Top Ten Names Born to Pitch
"Jay Hook, John Strike, Early Wynn, Mike Palm, Chief Bender, Darcy Fast, Rollie Fingers, Bill Hands, Bob Walk & Erik Plunk."

Kings of the Hill — Nolan Ryan with Mickey Herskowitz

"*The mark of a successful man is not what he takes out of life, but rather what he gives to it. Darcy Fast didn't give up on a dream: he simply pursued a different one that has had far greater meaning. This book is for all of us who face the challenge of determining who we are and what we are here to do.*"

Chris Sperry, Head Baseball Coach —
University of Portland

"*Darcy Fast is one of those guys who can walk into a room and be noticed. Not because he is self-promoting in any way, but because he displays a kind of quiet confidence that turns heads and inspires others to learn more. About life. About understanding where we have been and where we are going. About finding a place and a peace in this world that everyone, fundamentally, longs to discover.*

Darcy's story is the stuff of dreams. Dreams once realized, and then lost, and then found again. It is, in many ways, a narrative of what every boy growing up dreams, but cannot achieve. More importantly, though, his is a story that could be ours as well. And that's what makes this book a must read. Maybe, just maybe, by reading Darcy's story, you will find your own."

Jim Lyon, Senior Pastor — Senior Pastor,
Madison Park Church of God

Dedication

To A.J. & Ethel Fast—My parents, who are now with the Lord, and to their unified faith in their youngest son and their unwavering support of his dreams, which gave me the confidence and desire to find the things I do well. Thank you for your love and your Christian example to your family and to so many people.

Dad & Mom, this pitch is for you!

Acknowledgements

Winning baseball requires dedication and teamwork. When I became immersed in writing this book, I began to realize how many people have stood shoulder to shoulder with me. I want to express my admiration and gratitude for the contributions of these people:

Jonathan Kravetz —my assistant and avid Boston Red Sox fan, who caught the vision for this book and went to bat for *The Missing Cub* with his research and expertise. As I began recalling stories long forgotten, the direction of this book began changing, and you supported me through the entire process.

JoAnn Fast —My wife, my love, and my best friend. You shared my dreams when others doubted and have been my main cheerleader throughout my life. You are the one, without a doubt, that I come to and receive the best answers. You are the love of my life!

Chris and Brycen Fast—My two sons and their wonderful families—Dyan, McKailey, and Madison; Kami, Alyx and Taber. You are my great treasures from the Lord. By your lives, you validate what I believe and have taught throughout my life. Thank you for your great encouragement in writing this book.

Centralia Community Church of God—My wonderful church family. There are far too many to name and still have room in this book. Their devotion has been steadfast and essential. They have stood strong and their intercession has been deeply felt. May God bless your faithful hearts.

The Chicago Cubs—for their support in writing a positive book about baseball. Some day the Cubbies will win it all!

Hurricane Disaster Relief—Proceeds from the sale of this book will go to assist numerous churches and individuals with both emergency relief and long-term recovery through Compassionate Ministries. If you would like to help with hurricane relief in the Gulf States, you may give online with your credit card or send checks made payable to "Church of God Ministries", P.O. Box 2420, Anderson IN 46018-2420. Please write "Hurricane Relief, Project 45.04502 on your memo line.

Table of Contents

Foreword

I've known Darcy Fast for over 30 years. In the 70's, when I was a Trustee of Warner Pacific College, he was one of our notable students; in the 80's, as a Vice President at WPC, I knew him as the young senior pastor at Centralia Community Church of God, and even filled the pulpit for him while he enjoyed a sabbatical; and today as President at Warner Pacific, I know that Darcy is one of the college's strongest supporters. I've watched through the years as his roles have changed, always noting that through the early struggle he had with claiming his calling, his identity never wavered: Darcy is a son of the Church and devoted to Jesus Christ, his Savior and ours.

His desire from a young age to play baseball at the highest levels is a dream that is common to most of us. Who hasn't imagined playing in front of thousands of fans, striking out the star batter, sliding into home for the game winning run, and accepting the accolades? For many of us, that dream is never realized and we may wonder, "What if…?" In Darcy's case, his dream was realized, and yet he came to feel that it wasn't fulfilling enough for him.

Darcy made choices that sometimes bewildered even him, even though they felt right at the time. Coming to Warner Pacific College was not something that was in the mainstream of opinion about where he should go and what he should do. He struggled with that decision, and yet the opportunity to play at a higher level continued to follow him; God honored his choices. Even though he was drafted and could have played earlier, he chose to enroll at Warner Pacific and complete his degree — something not many young people would have the foresight to do. Thus, looking back through His perfect plan, God uniquely equipped Darcy to pursue his calling and honored his faithfulness.

Though Darcy's story is unique to him, there are so many elements that resonate strongly within all of us. The drive to be special and praiseworthy, the desire to fulfill God's plan for our lives, and the struggle with the paradox of God's calling versus our own plans are all themes that beat within our own hearts, too. I pray that his story will touch many lives and inspire people who are driven to excellence for God's kingdom, and I'm so thankful that Warner Pacific played such an important part in his life and the lives of so many others.

Dr. Jay A. Barber, Jr.
President, Warner Pacific College

Chapter 1

Introduction

I played major league baseball. I shook Ernie Banks' hand, I watched Billy Williams clout mammoth home runs, and I pitched against the Atlanta Braves when Hank Aaron and Joe Torre were in their prime. Leo Durocher, the sideshow performer turned manager of the Chicago Cubs, looked down his crooked nose at me and scowled. I was there, in 1968, sitting in the bullpen waiting anxiously for the next opportunity to pitch.

Some have called me *The Missing Cub,* the left-handed arm that might have helped stabilize the pitching staff in 1969. Maybe I could have been there in the eighth inning that year to snuff out a rally with a key strikeout. Or perhaps I could have started a handful of games, preserving the ragged arms in the bullpen late in the season. Maybe I was the piece of the puzzle that could have prevented one of the most famous collapses in baseball history. Or maybe not. But I understand why, when I begin to recount my favorite baseball stories, that the eyes of those listening get bright and curious. Baseball stories evoke memories of great plays and key hits. They raise the question that makes baseball America's favorite past time: what might have been?

That glitter is only part of my story. I went from a humble upbringing in Olympia, Washington to a brief career with the Chicago Cubs and then, finally, to a long and satisfying calling. That journey, from aspiring athlete to Christian minister, is the story underneath the story, and the one that I find fascinates listeners even more—how, they want to know, did I decide to walk away from the sport I loved? How did I find my place in the world when, in the beginning, it was not at all clear what I should be doing? How did I find my purpose in life?

I was born in 1947 in Dallas, Oregon, the second son of a church organist and a minister. I painted houses with my father, and learned to hang wallpaper to make extra money. I had a paper route, and my extra money was spent on baseball cards. My brother, Dallas, was extremely musical. He had perfect pitch and could sit down at a piano, hear a tune, and then perform it as if the song was just playing in his head. I had a brick for an ear. I was Darcy, the younger brother who didn't do too much. All that changed when I became involved in athletics.

I was bigger and lankier than the other children, and right away I could see I could do things that other kids couldn't. I could hit the ball a long way and I could throw it past every little leaguer in town. My folks were not sports people, but they were amused by my passion. My natural ability immediately gave me a lot of pleasure and a sense of pride, and convinced me that I didn't want to follow in my father's footsteps. I respected and loved him, but when I looked at our humble home, I wanted more. I wanted to be a star. I wanted to hear the thundering applause of thousands of adoring fans. The ministry, my father's vocation, meant sacrifice. I was already thinking, "No sacrifices for me."

I played every sport I could through high school, including football and basketball, and I excelled. But my heart was with baseball. I wanted to be the next Mickey Mantle or Whitey Ford. I wanted to wear pinstripes. Even in Washington, anyone who wanted to play professional baseball wanted to play for the Yankees. I was contacted in 1965—the year of the first Major League draft, and the year I graduated from high school. It was the most exciting phone call of my life: they were calling to say they were drafting me.

And I turned them down.

I was already searching for something deeper in my life, and I didn't want to lose my chance to go to college. The Yankees wanted me to play baseball full time. I was torn, but I had to follow my heart: I knew I could still make it to the majors after college and I'd been offered a scholarship to one of the best baseball schools in the country—Washington State University. I decided I would go there, get my education, and play Division 1 baseball.

I turned them down too.

Instead, I went to Warner Pacific College, where my girlfriend (and future wife) JoAnn was going, and where my brother and father had gone before me. There was little chance, once I made that decision, that I'd play professional baseball. I wasn't sure of my decision, but something about it just felt right. It might be hard for someone else to understand how I could come so close to my dream, only to let it pass me by, and sometimes even I'm amazed at the choices I made then. But I was still just a confused kid, feeling my way through life. I wanted to have options. A Christian college would give me that. It never entered my mind that I was going to become a minister.

Even though our college baseball team hardly ever took the field (we played just 15 games per season) I had some very impressive outings. After my sophomore year, my dream started to seem possible again. Scouts started buzzing around Warner Pacific, saying things like, *"This Fast guy is the real thing."* They couldn't believe a small Christian college could produce a major league pitcher, but they didn't care either—if you could throw, they wanted you. So the Cubs drafted me in the special phase of the amateur draft. Unlike the Yankees, they permitted me to finish college while I played ball. Incredibly, I was back on track. The Cubs even paid for the rest of my college education.

I went to Caldwell, Idaho in the Pioneer League my first summer and competed against guys from Division I schools. After receiving some great coaching, I began to do well, sometimes striking out 13 to 14 batters a game. I led the league in strikeouts and was named to the All Star team and was called up directly to Tacoma, the Triple-A club, right at the end of the season. I started the next year in Class-A ball and got called up to the Cubs in June of 1968.

I was poised to become a major part of the team in 1969, but circumstances got in the way. The Vietnam War was raging and I'd finished college, which meant I was eligible for the draft. I was lucky to get in the National Guard, but I had to attend basic training from July right through the end of the season, destroying my plans for a grand entry. The story of the 1969 Cubs has been told a thousand times: the team was leading the National League halfway through August, having a great year. And then they started to fall, and nothing seemed able to stop the momentum. That was hard on me, because I thought I could help. They needed pitching and there's no question in my mind that they would have called me back up. But it just wasn't meant to be.

In <u>Select Cubs Remain Memorable Footnotes</u>, Mike Murphy writes:

"Darcy Fast was a 6-foot 3-inch, left-handed pitcher who shot through the Cubs minor league system. He made it to Chicago mid-way through his second professional season. Tell me a better name for a pitcher, Bill Hands? Rollie Fingers? Jack Armstrong, Bob Walk? Give me Darcy Rae Fast anytime."

I still could have made my mark in 1970, but not long after that, I voluntarily retired from baseball as one of the youngest players in the history of Major League Baseball to do so. I began sensing that baseball just didn't seem to be the right direction for my life anymore, and I knew there were other things I needed to do. A lot of guys I played ball with during that era didn't have a college education. I saw too many who had absolutely nothing else they could do. There were a lot of guys who were really afraid of that. Don't misunderstand, however: I wasn't sure what shape my life would take, or what I wanted to do. I was just following the path that felt right, in spite of my doubts and fears. I tried business and teaching, but that wasn't satisfying. Finally, I came full circle and started the career that I'd wanted to avoid as a child.

I was first inspired to write this book by my family and some sports writers in Chicago. But when a young man came into my office one day asking for advice—how he could find God's true direction for his life—I realized my experiences may be of help. It's a question without an easy answer. But when I considered my own life, I could see that there was a particular arc, that I made choices, as unsure as I felt, that finally put me on the road to the ministry. I denied it, kicking and screaming, but I finally ended up where God intended. And what got me there was the simple faith that if I continued to pursue my dreams, whether in baseball, business, teaching or the ministry, I would fulfill my purpose. It wasn't the questions that got me there, finally, but the choices I made.

Chapter 2

Duke Fast

I wanted to be a baseball player as far back as I can remember. It was a pretty unlikely occupation for a kid growing up in a small town, and in a family that hardly knew a baseball from a football, but I didn't know better. And I didn't care to know better.

I grew up in a wonderful Christian family. My father, A.J. Fast, was a minister. He was a handsome man with dark, wavy hair, clear blue eyes, and large hands, like a catcher. He was quick and agile for someone 6'2" and an extremely hard worker. I remember watching him run up tall ladders with a bucket of paint in his hands without spilling a drop. Dad grew up in Saskatoon, Saskatchewan Canada, where he lived on a farm with his parents, eight brothers and three sisters. He jumped a freight train to the United States when he was thirty to be with family. He met my mother in Saskatoon when she was playing the piano in church. They hit it off quickly. Ethel Fast was also tall and slightly built, with a beautiful smile and long, slender hands and fingers. She was a great cook, and could whip up an apple pie or chocolate cake to beat the world's best pastry chefs.

My parents moved around a lot when they were first married because my father was the pastor of several different churches. His first church was in Milton-Freewater, Oregon, but not long after settling in that town, their first born son, Dale, died at birth. They moved again to Dallas, Oregon, where my father's brothers were living. My father founded the Church of God congregation there in an older house. He couldn't make enough money to support his family as a minister in the beginning, so he learned to paint houses and hang wallpaper to make ends meet. They named their second child Dallas, after the town, and I was born Darcy Rae Fast three years later.

We settled in Portland, Oregon for a short time. Dad attended Warner Pacific College there, which at that time was known as Pacific Bible College. He was the pastor of the Irving Park Church of God, a German congregation, and conducted the services entirely in German. Mom worked in the church, and Dad also had a weekly radio program in Portland called Wondrous Grace. We moved to LaGrande, Oregon when I was about six, and I spent kindergarten and first grade there. Dallas and I liked LaGrande because it was a small town and the members of the Pioneer Park Church of God, where Dad became a pastor, treated us very well.

When Dad became the pastor of the Church of God in Olympia, Washington, we lived in a little two bedroom yellow parsonage on North Tullis Street with a post and block foundation and an old oil stove. Wherever we lived, Mom transformed it into a home, decorating and fixing it up. I remember helping her wash and wax those ancient wooden floors. She'd get a little upset because, unfortunately, they didn't look much better after we cleaned them. The tiny congregation was in an old, dilapidated white building on Fourth Avenue. The building was eventually torn down and became part of the parking lot for the Olympian newspaper. I spent the next three years attending Roosevelt Grade School. The church eventually bought eighteen acres of ground in Lacey and built a beautiful church there on Ruddle Rd. and Lacey Blvd. We moved to Lacey the summer before I entered the sixth grade. It's a city now, but at that time Lacey wasn't incorporated, so it was simply a nice suburban area of Olympia.

My family and friends decided to drive over to watch me play baseball during my first professional season in Caldwell, Idaho, and on our way there, the car broke down miles away from any gas station. Dad got out of the car, laid his hands on the hood, and prayed that God would fix it. Dad's friends snickered a little, but when the car started they all stopped—they couldn't believe it. And, incredibly, they didn't have any more trouble with the car that day. Dad's faith in God was unshakable.

Dad really cared for people, too. He had a contagious laugh and people enjoyed being around him—he loved to tell stories. I remember the story he told me about his childhood on the farm. He said that one time he and his brother Casey were going to a dance in town and they wanted to make a big impression on the young ladies. They only had one pair of shoes between them, though. So Casey, his older brother, told him that they would share wearing them. Casey said, *"Abe, you can wear them walking into town."* And when they arrived at the dance, Casey said, *"OK Abe, now it's my turn."* So Casey got to wear the shoes during the entire dance, and when they were ready to leave, he said, *"OK Abe, now it's your turn to wear them home."* Dad laughed and said he didn't feel much like dancing that night.

On another occasion, he and his brothers decided that they would see if pigs could swim. Their parents were away in town, and so they picked up a pig and threw him in the well with a rope tied around him. Dad said, *"The pig swam like a rock and sank to the bottom of the well."* When his parents got home, they were all in big trouble.

Dad was also a disciplinarian who believed in hard work. One afternoon, while I was painting a house with him, he told me specifically not to get paint on the window trim. I didn't pay attention to what I was doing, naturally, and I got paint everywhere. He pulled me aside and said, *"Darcy, you know, we grow old too soon, and smart too late. Do it all over again, and do it right!"*

Dad expected his two sons to work and earn money for ourselves, so Dallas and I became very industrious at a young age. We helped Dad paint houses and hang wallpaper. We sold Christmas cards, had paper routes, and sold all-occasion cards (a variety of birthday, anniversary, sympathy and holiday cards). Sometimes we went door-to-door selling packages of seeds for people to buy for their vegetable gardens. I had my first paper route when I was nine years of old, which was unheard of then, and I was named the second-best among seventy-seven Daily Olympian paper boys in the city in 1956. I got my picture in the paper (a shot of me receiving a trophy and shaking hands with a local businessman) for the first time in my life.

Mom helped my Dad with the ministry and played piano in church. She was also a pillar of strength. She developed rheumatoid arthritis when Dallas and I were young and it caused her a great deal of pain. Her hands and feet were especially crippled. Her friends marveled at the fact that she never complained about it. Just watching her taught me as much about life and courage as anything anyone has ever said to me.

Even though our lives centered around the church, my parents gave Dallas and I the freedom to decide what we were going to do with our lives. They raised us in a Christian home and yes, they hoped someday we would follow in their steps, but they didn't push it. We got a lot of love and support for everything we wanted to do. And I knew I *definitely* didn't want to be a minister. I had a passion from the day I was born: I didn't want to be a fireman, or a doctor or a lawyer. I wanted to be a baseball player.

I would scrounge around our house, searching for anything round I could throw or toss—if there was a ball, then you'd find me hitting it with a bat or bouncing it off the roof of our house. I spent most of my childhood outside playing football, basketball or baseball with my buddies. I tagged along with Dallas a lot, too, so I got to play with older kids. That probably helped me develop my athletic skills a little faster.

I got interested in baseball by watching games on television. I began to live and breathe the sport. Some of my earliest memories are of pro ballplayers. During the summer between fourth and fifth grades, I won a trip with other Daily Olympian paperboys to watch the Seattle Rainiers play at Sicks Stadium. Vada Pinson fouled a ball into the stands that hit me in the leg, and I felt rather honored. Years later, I played against him when he was playing center field for the Cincinnati Reds and I was with the Cubs.

Before long, Dad and Mom knew how much I loved playing baseball. When I was eight years old, Dad came to my room and said, *"Darcy, I've got a surprise for you! We're going to see an exhibition game between the Portland Beavers and the St. Louis Cardinals."* I was excited beyond words because it meant I'd get to see Stan Musial play. When we arrived at old Multnomah Stadium and sat down on the green bleacher seats along right field, I couldn't believe how many people there were—I'd never seen that many people in one place in my life. Even though we were sitting far from the field, I spotted Stan the Man right away. I was impressed with his gray uniform and the red Cardinal on his jersey. The fans gave him a standing ovation when he came to the plate, and I jumped up, breathless, with the rest of them. That season, 1955, he batted .319 with 33 homeruns and 108 RBI's.

The Yankees were my favorite team because they were on TV almost every Saturday, and they seemed to win the World Series every year. I loved listening to Phil Rizzuto and Dizzy Dean broadcast the games, and before long my favorite players were Mickey

Mantle, Roger Maris, Bobby Richardson, Whitey Ford, and Tony Kubek. I remember Don Larsen pitching his perfect game—the only one ever pitched in a World Series game. It was Game 5 against the Brooklyn Dodgers on October 8, 1956. He needed just 97 pitches, and only one Dodger batter, Pee Wee Reese, was able to muster even a three ball count. I remember Mickey Mantle made a spectacular running, one-handed catch in center field to steal a hit from Gil Hodges. And I felt like I was Yogi Berra when he jumped into Larsen's arms after he struck out Dale Mitchel for the final out. Even now, there have only been 17 perfect games in the history of baseball. I thought to myself, *"Some day I would love to play for the Yankees and wear those pinstriped uniforms!"* I had no idea then that I would be drafted by the Yankees, and that someday I would play with Don Larsen. When I got the chance, I asked him about his perfect game. He told me, *"Darcy, I've never had that kind of control in any game that I pitched in my life."*

There were skeptics about my aspirations. There always are. When I was eleven years old and playing little league baseball in Lacey, one of my coaches gave me a ride home after a practice. I was sitting in the back seat with his son when he asked me what I wanted to do when I grew up.

"I want to be a major league baseball player," I said.

"Do you know any professional baseball players?" he asked.

"Well, no," I replied.

"I don't know of anyone in Olympia, Lacey or Tumwater who ever played professional ball," he said. *"Not many kids get a chance*

to be professional baseball players, so you'd better plan to do some-thing different with your life."

It hadn't even occurred to me that I might not grow up to be a major leaguer. But the coach's skepticism only made me more determined than ever. I told my Dad what the coach had told me, and he said, *"Darcy, just keep following your dream. God has a great plan and purpose for you life."*

In fifth grade I had another paper route, and when collection time came around and people asked me who to make the checks out to, I had a special answer for them.

"Make it out to Duke Fast," I'd tell them. Duke Snider, the sensational centerfielder for the Brooklyn Dodgers, was my favorite player.

On pay day, I would take my paper route money and buy baseball cards at Apex Grocery store on 4th Avenue in Olympia. It was a small, old building with blue faded paint and creaky wood floors, and it was located across the street from Ralph's Thriftway, a large brick grocery store. I would go into the Thriftway to get a Green River soda during the summer and sit on the fountain chairs, turning in circles. Apex was at the top of a hill, naturally—besides baseball cards, they also sold novelty items like chocolate covered ants, chocolate grasshoppers and canned rattlesnake meat. I tried the chocolate grasshoppers once—they tasted a little like shaved coconut, and I didn't like that either, so I had more fun trying them on my friends. Apex had the best selection of Topps Baseball Cards in town. I would meet my friends there and sit outside, trading for our favorite players. One pack of cards cost five cents, and I usually saved up enough to purchase several packs. I loved the smell of the bubblegum when you opened the package, and I chewed it as I went through the cards. Whenever I got a Mantle, Mays, Snider, Musial or Aaron card, if I had it already, I could trade it for three or four other cards. The players I didn't like ended up on the spokes of my green Schwinn bike and provided me, I thought, with extra power (and noise) on my way home.

I remember when I began to realize that the players on the cards were real. One day I went into Apex and the owner, who'd gotten to know me, asked, *"What are you doing with all those cards, kid?"*

I said, *'When I grow up, I'm going to play baseball with these guys, and I need to know who they are."*

It didn't matter to me that no one else in the family understood baseball. I was strong-willed and independent. I joined Little League as soon as I was old enough, and I proudly wore the t-shirts and caps they issued us. I continued to work, of course, even though I was playing sports—I kept my paper route for about five years, and before I could practice I had to deliver about 125 newspapers. There wasn't much time left over after my job and baseball.

I got my first lefty glove the year I played my first year of organized baseball, in Portland. I was in second grade. Dad ordered the glove from the Montgomery Ward catalog, and that immediately made it easier to catch. Before then I'd used only righty gloves on my left hand—I had to catch the ball with my left, quickly remove the glove and ball with my right, and transfer the ball back to my left so I could throw.

I played for Roosevelt Grade School my second year. I was so excited to bring my new green baseball shirt and baseball cap home after practice that I immediately told Mom she had to iron the "R" on the cap that they'd given us. The next day, when I took my baseball cap to practice, I was horrified to see that she had ironed the "R" on the bill of the cap! My mother knew even less about sports than my father, and she didn't know where the letter was supposed to go—she just put it where it made sense to her. My teammates thought it was very funny. For that whole season no one could tell what team I played for unless they were tall enough to look down on my cap.

My first little league coach decided to make me a first baseman because I was tall and a good target for the infielders. To my delight, I made the All-Star team in that season and I was really excited—instead of just a baseball cap and t-shirt, I was going to get to wear a complete uniform. We were called the Skyway All-Stars. I couldn't wait to get home and try on the white flannel pants with the red lettering on the jersey. I had one big problem, though—I had no idea how to put on the red and white stirrups. By that point, I knew not to ask my parents, so I figured I was clever enough to figure it out for myself. After puzzling over it for a few minutes, I decided the best way to wear them was between my toes. It wasn't very comfortable, but I didn't know any better. When I went to my first game, I knew something was wrong right away, because the top of my socks ended just above my ankle and all the other kids' socks went up their calves. I knew I wasn't *that* tall, and I finally figured it out—stirrups *do not* go between the big toe and the second toe. The other kids on the team got a good laugh at me. My new coaches weren't too impressed either, because I never got to play in a single game. Of course, some of those games were played on Sundays, and there was no way I was going to play then. In our family, Sunday was for church—not for baseball.

I was bigger, taller and more athletic than most of the kids I was competing against. I never thought much about that until my coach brought me home after practice one evening and told my parents that he was going to need a copy of my birth certificate to prove to the other coaches that I was as old as I was saying. We thought it was funny. From that point on, I kept a copy of my birth certificate in my back pocket when I was playing ball. Opposing coaches would often ask to see it before games.

Philippians 4:13

One evening in Olympia, we were having a special church meeting with Rev. Wendel Wallace that I was expected to attend. I had a ball game that night and didn't think my dad was going to let me play.

"Darcy," he said, *"I can't be at your game, but I want you to play today and remember this verse: "I can do everything through*

him who gives me strength." Dad said, *"Remember—God can help you be a good baseball player."* I hit a home run that night, and I was extremely excited. After the game, I told my folks what had happened and they were excited for me, too.

I didn't get to play ball with my father as much as I would have liked growing up, but when I think about it now, it was OK. My parents supported my love for baseball, and even though they couldn't attend all my games, I understood—church was our priority, not baseball. What they were doing was more important, and I knew it. Being a pastor just wasn't *my* dream. I would think, *"God, I don't want to be a minister, but if you will help me become a great baseball player, I'll give you all the credit."* I was glad my parents didn't pressure me into playing sports the way some parents do today. I had more fun without the pressure because Dad and Mom taught me there were more important things in life.

Playing sports gave me a lot of confidence, which is something I needed at the time. My mother wanted Dallas and I to learn to play music, but I wasn't very good at it. Everyone else in the family could either sing or play a musical instrument. In fact, my mother and father made and recorded a number of songs on the old 33s. Music was a big part of our family.

Music came naturally to Dallas—he had perfect pitch—and it made me a little envious. He could sit down and play the organ easily, and he got a lot of recognition for it. He didn't even need sheet music. When I was just a young boy, one of our church members came up to me after the service and said, *"Darcy, don't you wish that you could play like your brother?"* That hurt, because I wanted to—I just didn't have the talent or desire. My mother sat down on the piano bench every day and gave me lessons, but it just wouldn't take. One time, she got so frustrated that she got up and went into her bedroom so I wouldn't see her crying. But I knew I'd disappointed her. I took trumpet lessons. I took violin lessons. I took cello lessons. I took lessons in just about every instrument you can think of, and I didn't master a single one. I just really wanted to be outside playing ball.

I was very good at baseball, though, and I began to like the attention. It seemed that all of the coaches wanted me on their teams, and that made me want to be even better. It wasn't just baseball, either—I was pretty good at just about every sport I tried.

Unfortunately, my dream of playing baseball almost came to end before it started. I was in the seventh grade at Lacey Grade School and in order to play sports there, all the kids had to pass a physical exam. I must have seen doctors before that, but I don't remember any of them. I remember seeing Dr. Lux at the Memorial Clinic. After the exam he asked my father and I to come into his office. He said that he'd discovered a heart murmur and that he could not allow me to play. He said he was going to re-examine me the following week, but he was pretty sure he'd gotten it right. It was a torturous week, but I was convinced that he had to be wrong. After the second exam, however, he said with a grim certainty that he could not allow me to play. There was only one recourse left, he said: we could go to the University of Washington Hospital to get another opinion.

I was devastated, and I felt like a very important part of my life had come to an end. My family didn't have medical insurance and I assumed my folks couldn't afford to take me to get an expensive examination. A couple days later at breakfast, however, Dad said, *"Mom and I know how much this means to you, so we've decided we want you to have the examination."* I was happy and grateful, but I still figured I wouldn't pass the test. The drive from Olympia to Seattle a couple of weeks later seemed especially long. Dad was not familiar with the area and he asked Wilbur Skaggs, a pastor in Seattle, to meet us and drive us to the hospital. Before we got out of the car, Pastor Skaggs told me that his church was praying for me. I was grateful to know that so many people were concerned about my future.

The hospital doctors and staff were friendly, and they helped me relax. I went through stress tests, EKG's and a few other exams. When the doctors finished, they called us into a conference room. One stood up and said, *"We've given Darcy a thorough examination and he does have a functional heart murmur, but we believe he will outgrow it. Based upon his results, we see no reason why he shouldn't be able to participate in athletics without any limitations."* I was so happy that I cried and hugged my father. I realized that my dream of playing baseball was still possible.

Fouts and McCallum

When Dallas and I got a little older and started taking an interest in girls, my father would often say, *"Remember boys—love many, trust few, but always paddle your own canoe."*

In ninth grade at Chinook Middle School (the first year they opened that school), I met my future wife, JoAnn. She and some other girls were cheerleaders, and they were riding on the bus with the football team to cheer at our first football game. JoAnn sat in the seat in front of me. We got to talking and I immediately liked her. I don't remember anything about the game that day, whether we won or lost, but I do remember having a ball getting to know JoAnn. She was easy to talk to, and very pretty. She later became a cheerleader in high school and college, and today I tell people that we got married because I wanted to make her my cheerleader for life.

JoAnn's family did not attend church, and that sometimes presented a little bit of a problem. My parents expected me to date the "right" kind of girl, but later in high school, when her family started attending church and my parents got to know them, they felt very good about her. They loved JoAnn. When she told her Dad that she liked a boy whose father was a pastor he wasn't very impressed, either—his best friend was a PK (Preacher's Kid), and together they got into more trouble than anyone else at their school. I didn't know this when I introduced myself to him after a high school basketball game, but he must have been favorably impressed, as I later developed a very close friendship with her parents.

JoAnn and I dated all through high school, although we had an on-and-off relationship, especially during my senior year. A lot of colleges and pro scouts were interested in me, and by then I was feeling a lot of pressure. I wasn't sure what I was going to do after high school. But JoAnn and I loved each other, and that's why, in the end, we got married.

I had two incredible coaches in high school: Archie McCallum and Jim Fouts. Without either one of them, I doubt I would have made it to the major leagues. That's how much of a difference they made to me. They helped me throughout high school, taught me many things about sports, and helped to develop my character and leadership abilities.

Archie McCallum was my basketball coach. He was a disciplinarian, like my dad. He knew I had a lot of athletic ability, but he never let me get a big head about it. He was a little like legendary coach Bobby Knight: he pushed his players to become the best they could possibly be.

When Coach McCallum told you to jump, you jumped and didn't ask him how high. One day, he didn't like the way we were practicing. We were not very focused and were playing sloppy, so he pulled the starting five off the court and said, *"If you don't want to take the game more seriously, just go take a shower and go home — and I don't want to see you coming back in the gym again today."* He knew we'd have to go the locker room to change, and that the only way back out was through the gym. He didn't care, because he was disgusted with our effort. The only way we could get out of the locker room was to climb through a window above the door and slide out. And we did, because no one wanted to face Coach McCallum. He got his message across, though, and I was grateful. *"If I'm going to play for him,"* I thought, *"I'd better take this game seriously."* It was a great lesson.

I went into his class one day after school to ask him for my practice gear, since the football season was just over. There were rules for when you could and couldn't collect your gear, but I was feeling pretty good, I suppose, because I'd just been named an All-American basketball player the previous year and I was looking forward to another good basketball season. He said, *"Darcy, you'll get your practice gear when everyone else gets their gear—when you make the team."* With that statement, I knew he was sending a message—I was going to have to work hard, just like every other year, and I wasn't going to get any special treatment.

I learned as much from Coach McCallum after practice as I did during it. He often gave me a ride home and we'd talk about my future. He'd tell me the things I needed to do to get to the next level, and it often had more to do with me as an individual than it did my athleticism. "Darcy," he once said, "The only thing that will keep you from reaching your goals will be you." I expected a lot out of myself then, and if I didn't do well or if something wasn't coming easily, I would get down on myself. *"That'll get in your way,"* Coach would say. *"Just stay positive, work hard, and you'll make it."* I trusted Coach McCallum completely, and I knew his criticism was never intended to put me down. In high school I could be my own worst enemy, so I needed his support.

In my senior year, I was left off of the All-Conference basketball team, after making it during my sophomore and junior years. It made no sense, and I was pretty upset. I led the Seamount League in rebounding and scoring, and had been selected to the non-tournament All-State team. I was named a high school All-American and was rated as one of the top 500 basketball players in the United States. How could I be left off the All-Conference team?

When my folks heard the news they asked Coach McCallum over to our house. He came in and sat down in our living room, and he took most of the responsibility himself. He said that there were some coaches who had it out for him. *"It's all about personalities,"* he said. *"People feel a lot of jealousy when somebody like Darcy really excels. He will be a better person for this and I believe he's got some bigger things ahead of him in sports."*

I realized then that it wasn't only other players, but also opposing coaches, who might want to see me fail. People can get jealous of another's success. I'd made All-State and All-American, but I didn't make All-Conference. It was crazy.

Jim Fouts was my football and baseball coach; he was a legend in those parts. He coached baseball at North Thurston High for 37 years with an amazing record of 535 Wins and 223 Losses. His incredible career included 15 League Championships, 2 Regional Titles, 2 State Runner-up Finishes, and 1 Fourth Place Finish. Coach Fouts was inducted into the Washington State Baseball Hall of Fame in 1988 and was named Washington State Baseball Coach of the Year in 1976 and 1987. He was also inducted into the Washington Babe Ruth Hall of Fame in 1988, the St. Martins University Hall of Fame in 1991, the Washington State Football Hall of Fame, and was honored by having the North Thurston High School Football Field named "Fouts Field" in 2001. He passed away in November 9, 2004.

Coach Fouts was first and foremost a gentleman, and expected his players to play the same way. He would not tolerate any unsportsmanlike conduct from his players. He saw that I had the ability and potential to turn pro, but he treated me like everyone else—he wanted me to focus on playing high school ball and helping the team win the conference championship. He didn't want me thinking too much about the future; he knew that would take care of itself after I graduated.

I found out how interested pro teams were in me one afternoon, however. Coach asked me to go into his office to get him some papers and I saw, on top of his desk, a letter from the St. Louis Cardinals. It was just sitting there, exposed. A Cardinal scout wanted to come and watch me play. I was really excited, but when I saw the letter, I was afraid to ask Coach Fouts about it. I thought he was going to think I was nosy. I also didn't want to think about what was going on. I trusted him to take care of things.

I did notice, though, that scouts started attending many of our games. During that era, they didn't have radar guns like they do today, but they could tell a kid's potential just by watching him. I didn't really start pitching a lot until I was a junior in high school, but I didn't care which position they wanted me to play—I just wanted to be a professional baseball player. If they wanted me to be a pitcher, that would have been fine, and if they wanted me to be a first baseman, that would have been fine, too.

After a while, it became obvious who the scouts were there to see. Even though they usually didn't talk to me, I knew. After one of our practices late in the season of my senior year, Eddy Taylor, a Yankees scout, asked if I could stay after practice so he could see me hit and pitch off the mound. He must have been impressed, although he didn't say so then. Babe Barberis, who scouted for the Pittsburgh Pirates, also came by to watch me one afternoon.

Later, I remember Coach Fouts coming to my house to talk to my parents.

"Mr. and Mrs. Fast," he said, *"Darcy's going to have a lot of decisions to make about his future this year, and we want to help him make the right ones."* He continued, *"I'm not sure you understand how many college scholarship offers he's going to get and the number of professional scouts that will be watching him play."*

Drafted by the Yankees

My senior year baseball season got off to a flying start. I pitched a no-hitter against Sumner High School and struck out thirteen Spartan hitters. I also went two-for-five at the plate, including a triple and a double, and I drove in three runs. I was chosen for the All-State game that year, which was a big thrill, although it didn't turn out as great at I would have liked. The game was played in Tacoma at Heidelberg Field, and the best players in the state were there. I was a pitcher and first baseman, but the coaches wouldn't let me play either of those positions. They stuck me in the outfield, and in the second game I wasn't even in the lineup. Eddy Taylor and some of the other scouts came over to our dugout and asked why I wasn't playing.

The coach said, *"He's finished for today,"* and that was it. The scouts couldn't figure it out, and I couldn't understand why they weren't letting me play. It was probably because I was from a small community that wasn't known for its baseball like the bigger schools in the area were. The scouts knew me, of course, but the coaches didn't and they wanted to feature their guys. I was very disappointed.

My disappointment didn't last long. Two days later was the first major league draft. I received a telegram from the Yankees—they wanted me! They had drafted me as a first- baseman. I celebrated with my parents, and then drove to the high school to tell Coach Fouts. He was in a teachers' meeting when I got there, so I paced until he got out. When I showed him the telegram he gave me a big hug.

"I was pretty sure this was going to happen, Darcy," he said. *"I wanted to talk to you so much about this over these past few months, because so many professional scouts have contacted me. This is a*

great opportunity for you." Incredibly, there were only two players from that all-star game who ended up getting drafted that year.

Next I went to find Coach McCallum. He was excited, too, and very happy for me. Interestingly, he said, *"I never thought you'd make it as a pitcher, Darcy. You're a better first baseman."* Of course, when I finally did make it to the majors, it was as a pitcher.

About a week later, Eddy Taylor called and asked to come over to discuss signing a contract with the Yankees. Mr. Taylor had been in organized baseball since 1921, played for the White Sox and Boston Braves, and had coached in the Pacific Coast League for 14 years. He'd even played and coached for legendary manager Casey Stengle. He'd been scouting since 1951, and spent the previous four years with the Yankees, so he really knew baseball. I'll never forget the day he parked his new, black Fleetwood Cadillac on our driveway. I couldn't believe it—I'd never seen a car that big or that beautiful in my life. He got out of the car, came inside, and told us what it was like to play ball for the Yankees. He gave us all kinds of literature. He told me I had been drafted by the Yankees in the 7th round, and that I was one of 469 high school players drafted in the first major league baseball draft.

At that point, there was nothing I wanted to do more than play baseball for the New York Yankees. It was my dream—every boy's dream—coming true. And yet, I didn't sign the contract. Looking back, this seems incredible, but I was beginning to think more about my future, and I wanted to make sure this is what I should do.

I knew that the odds against anyone getting a chance to play professional were great, and that I could be making a big mistake. In his book, Comeback, Dave Dravecky used an analogy to describe how fortunate he was to be able to play professional baseball in the major leagues. He asked readers to imagine a baseball stadium filled with little leaguers, each wearing a uniform and a glove, fervently wishing to be invited down to the field to play. Now, out of those thousands of kids, only one gets to play. Just imagine—out of 10,000 little leaguers, only one will eventually get the opportunity to play professionally. Here are some figures from Nearly the Greatest that will serve as an estimate of today's odds: based on the number of players actually playing at each of these levels, and the number of new openings in the major leagues in the early 1990s, it was estimated that of all the boys playing high school baseball then, only 4.2% would move on to play college baseball. About two-tenths of 1% would go directly to play professional baseball, almost all of whom would be assigned to Class A, the lowest minor league classification. Of those college baseball players who were still playing at the end of their fourth year in college, only about 1% would become professional baseball players. Again, most of these players would be assigned to Class A. The road from Class A to the major leagues is often long and hard. Few make it, and of those who do, a typical Major League career is one to three years.

I had figured out at that point that I really wanted to go to college and only play baseball in the summer. But the Yankees didn't want me to attend college. I thought, *"It's one thing to sign with the*

Yankees, but it's another to give up my education." I told Mr. Taylor that I had to think about signing the contract and, in the meantime, went off to play American Legion ball for the Colonels in Centralia, Washington.

The coach of the Legion team was Ed Wheeler, who had played for the Cleveland Indians. He was a legend in that area, and the field where we played is now named after him. They got me a job as a sleeper for the fire department. Sleepers live at the station, and in exchange for free lodging, you have to go out on any calls that come up while you're there. Lucky for me, there was only one fire I had to help with that summer. To support myself, I also worked for the City of Centralia in the road department. I kept plenty busy.

Centralia was a very close community, and I was from Lacey, about twenty-five miles away. That made me a stranger to the people of the town. They had their own baseball program, and people in the town expected to see their own kids playing—to them I was just some kid taking a position away from one of the locals. That was a very frustrating time, but coach Wheeler was happy to have me on the team and understood the pressure I was feeling about signing a professional contract.

Eddy Taylor often came to our games to watch me play and was still after me to sign a contract. It didn't take long for him to begin irritating Ed Wheeler. One day he'd had enough, and threw Mr. Taylor out of the ballpark—with orders for him never to come back! I was really embarrassed, because Eddy Taylor was an extremely nice man who was only trying to do his job. After that experience, I wondered if I'd blown my chance to ever play in the pros.

I played well in Centralia, even though there was a lot of pressure on me. People in town hardly knew me, so instead of introducing me like the other players when I came to bat for the first time, the announcer said, *"Now batting, Darcy Fast, the 7th round draft pick of the Yankees."* I was hitting cleanup in that first game and luckily drove a bases loaded home run over the right center field fence, over 405 feet away. That took a little pressure off.

God's Purpose

Why didn't I sign with the Yankees right away? I still ask myself that question. Part of me wanted to play baseball and do nothing else. The other part of me knew that college was very important. I was growing up, and I saw that becoming an adult came with responsibilities. I began to wonder what I was meant to do in life, though I couldn't see anything past baseball.

In my senior year, my mother got very sick, and that really got me thinking. It was a Friday afternoon, and I had just finished putting on my football gear when my father walked into the locker room. He had never been there before, so I knew something was wrong. He was normally upbeat and optimistic, but today he looked sad and serious. He told me I needed to go with him right away to St. Peter Hospital. Our doctor had discovered that my mother had a malignant tumor in her breast and in the lymph nodes under her left arm. They had to perform a radical mastectomy, but there was no guarantee this would save her. It felt like someone had kicked me in the stomach. I was shocked. By then Coach Fouts and Coach McCallum had seen us. I started getting emotional when I told them the news, and then I saw a side of them that I'd never seen before. They reassured me and told me to take whatever time I needed—if I didn't feel like playing in the next game, it was perfectly fine. Their understanding and support was unbelievable. They were already great men to me, but they stood even taller that day.

I didn't know what to say to my mother when I walked into the hospital room to visit that first time. I stood shaking my head, wondering how God could allow something like this to happen to such a wonderful person.

She said, *"Honey, don't you worry. God is going to take care of me."* As our family prayed together around her hospital bed, I knew there was more to life than just sports. The surgery went well, and Mom completely recovered. We were relieved and my faith was greatly strengthened.

Chapter 3

Baseball or College

After agonizing over my decision all summer, I finally decided to enroll at Washington State University and play for legendary coach "Bobo" Brayton. I talked with Dale Ford, one of my high school's greatest athletes, who played for WSU in the College World Series that year. He told me that Coach Brayton was looking forward to having me on his team, and that it would be a great opportunity to further my baseball career. That meant I wasn't going to sign with the Yankees, after all. Instead, I signed a national letter of intention and got a full-ride scholarship. Coach Brayton wanted to know whether or not I was definitely going, because if I wasn't, he wanted to divide my scholarship between three other players.

I planned to attend WSU, but something special happened three weeks before college was supposed to start. Dr. Louis Gough invited me to visit Warner Pacific College in Portland, Oregon and have dinner with him at his home. He was the president of the school and was interested in me attending the college because my father and brother were both alumni. I knew there was little baseball there, but my priorities were changing, and JoAnn was also planning to attend Warner Pacific.

Dr. Gough told me he was planning to lead the college in relocating the campus to California. It would be an exciting time in the history of the school, and I had the chance to be a part of it. I believed the college could strengthen my Christian faith and my life. I thought, "If God still wants me to be a professional baseball player, it can still happen." So I decided a week before classes started to attend Warner Pacific College. That was one of the most critical decisions of my life. There were many people who said I was crazy to walk away from the Yankees and Washington State. I can see why they thought that, but I was still searching, like everyone else, for direction in my life. God had given me the ability to play baseball, but for what reason?

There were many factors that played into my decision to attend Warner Pacific, but I remember one particular conversation I had with Ron Patti, a highly respected youth minister, that made a big difference. In my senior year of high school, Ron and Carolyn Patti came to Olympia to speak at a youth rally. They were also ministers of music at the First Church of God in Phoenix, Arizona, and the parents of Sandi Patty, who later went on to win many Grammy Awards and was inducted in the Gospel Music Hall of Fame. Ron and Carolyn were outstanding musicians and had a long career singing together and with the Christian Brothers Quartet. They even performed at the White House for President Eisenhower, while playing and singing for Fred Warring and the Pennsylvanians.

Ron came to my high school football game the night before the rally. After the game, I got to meet and talk to him, and I began to tell him about the decision I was struggling with: to play professional baseball or go to WSU and play Division 1 baseball. In high school, Ron had an offer to play pro baseball himself, and he'd turned down a football scholarship at the University of Oklahoma. Instead, he attended Anderson College, a Christian school in Anderson, Indiana. I was surprised. I asked him why he'd made that choice, and I'll never forget his answer.

He said, *"Darcy, I believe I could have been a successful quarterback at Oklahoma or played professional baseball. But I attended Anderson College to help me figure out my life, and I have never regretted it. Remember, the most important thing is to find God's purpose for your life."*

Warner Pacific

Warner Pacific College is a Christian liberal arts college, located on the hillside of Mount Tabor in southeast Portland. The student body had about 600 students, and there were about fifteen students for every professor—a class ratio that I really appreciated. I also noticed that the professors at Warner Pacific took a personal interest in their students. Many could have been teaching at larger colleges and universities, but they were there because they were committed to Christian higher education and wanted to teach at a Christian school.

The Warner Pacific Knights competed in the National Association of Intercollegiate Athletics (NAIA) and in a Christian collegiate league in the Pacific Northwest. Although Warner Pacific had intercollegiate athletics — basketball, baseball, tennis, track and field, and wrestling — it was best known for its religion, psychology, music, and education majors. I was glad to attend a school where the students got to know their professors personally, and one where I would find a place that was compatible to my life and faith. I enjoyed the faculty and student body, and I figured that playing sports there would just be an added bonus.

I loved the beautiful campus, and JoAnn and I would spend our spare moments going on long walks around the grounds and to the city park above the school. We talked about our aspirations a lot on those strolls, and our love for each other grew deeper. JoAnn was selected to be a basketball cheerleader along with Cheryl Warren, Vicki Roller, Joy White and Janet Reiboldt. Janet became a lifetime friend and they shared many great times together. One winter day, JoAnn, Janet, my teammate Kent Walton and I borrowed a friend's car to drive to Timberline Lodge on Mt. Hood for a fun time in the snow. The car was an old 1952 Oldsmobile, and it wasn't in the best of conditions. The front seat would not lock and the tires were bald, but that didn't keep four college kids from having a great time together. Coming down the mountain that evening with bald tires and no chains was a different story. The roads were icy, and we slid more than we drove down the mountain. The only way we could get down was to slide it into the high snow drifts to cushion the car down the road. It was quite an experience. We finally made it back to the college, but our friend's car was never the same.

It seemed like we were always short of money in those days, so whenever one of us could afford it, we would walk down to Candy's Restaurant on Division St. and order their famous grilled tuna sandwich. It was delicious. Candy's was a hang out for other college students as well, a place to relax.

The professors at Warner Pacific made a dramatic impact upon our lives. Dr. Wilma Perry was my psychology professor, and after taking her classes, I was sure I wanted to major in psychology. She really inspired me, and I looked forward to what she said in every class. I remember sitting in her class one day when she was lecturing on faith as a powerful tool for our lives. She said that faith is the ability to believe something before you see it. She used the example of Joshua, who had been leading the children of Israel to the Promised Land when the Lord told him to take the city of Jericho by marching around the walls of the city. On the seventh day, Joshua said, "Okay, ready, now… shout and blow the trumpets, the battle is won and the city is ours." Before a word was said, or before one blast had sounded from the horns, Joshua made a statement of faith. He had God's promise before he experienced the results. The people shouted, the priests blew the trumpets, and the walls fell flat to the ground. The Israelites leaped over the rubble and took the city. Dr. Perry said something that day that really stuck with me, "When was the battle won? Not when the trumpets sounded; not when the people shouted; not when the march started or even when they invaded the city. The victory came in advance when Joshua told them, 'The city is ours.'" She continued, "When you hear about the power of faith, don't dismiss it too quickly. It is the strength that allows you to achieve the impossible and reach the unattainable in your life."

Another professor I admired was our biological sciences professor, Dr. Oliver Titrud. He had such a passion for his work that at times he would have you either laughing or crying during his class. We learned anatomy by dissecting human cadavers, as Dr. Titrud believed that textbook pictures were not the same as the real thing. He was right. When he showed us the carotid artery, he said, "Men, never wear your shirts or ties too tight because it causes hypertension—always be able to get two fingers between your shirt collar and your neck." Another time when he was teaching a unit on health and nutrition, he said, "Ladies, every time you bake your husband a cake you're putting a nail in his coffin." He was referring to the amount of sugar we take into our bodies. Dr. Titrud was ahead of his time with many of his teachings.

I enjoyed my college experiences, but I'd given up hope of ever playing professional baseball at that point. What chance did I have of getting noticed playing for a small, Christian school in the Pacific Northwest? What scout was going to look for a player in a small Christian conference? None, I figured. But I'd made up my mind. I decided to major in education, play basketball and baseball at Warner Pacific, and never look back. As soon as I started playing sports, however, I realized that there were quite a few talented athletes there. Our basketball team included the tallest twin players in the country, George and Pat Nolan, who were both 6'8" centers. Guards Kent Walton and Dave Dougherty were smart and savvy, and forwards Gary Moore, Ron Kruse, and center Jerry Tange were also solid, intelligent players.

The coach of our basketball and baseball teams was Gary Aved. He was also the athletic director. Coach Aved work tirelessly to bring recognition to our athletic programs.

Compared to most colleges, we never took the field. We played fifteen baseball games a season while most played around sixty, and we played small schools, such as George Fox, Oregon Tech, Northwest Christian College, Concordia College, and Cascade College. It was easy for me to excel, but our team also had some other ballplayers that could have played at bigger schools, but chose Warner Pacific instead. I don't know if they could have gone pro, but they certainly had enough talent to play someplace besides Warner Pacific College. We shared a bond in that we were all there for something besides sports, and we recognized foremost the value of a Christian education. We won the Willamette Christian College Conference in both basketball and baseball, and surprised a lot of people in non-conference games.

Our baseball team had two good receivers in Dan Kaiser and LeRoy Tucker, who understood the game; infielders Bill and Rick Dunn, shortstop Frank Martinolich and Dave Schwartz were also good infielders; Kent Walton, Kent McLaughlin and Ralph Crane played capably in the outfield; the pitching was handled by Gary Moore, John Thomas, and myself. We didn't have our own baseball field, so we used the Portland City Parks as our home field. Our baseball team played and upset Lewis and Clark College—they were one of the top NAIA schools at the time—in an exhibition game my freshman year. They probably figured they'd come in and just whip us. I was the starting pitcher and in five innings (the full length of the exhibition game), I struck out eight, surrendered only two hits, and didn't give up a run. It was a great tune-up for our league games, but I was little upset over an article that appeared in the newspaper the next day entitled: "Fast's Fastballs: Sermon on the Mound." The writer didn't have his facts straight regarding my intentions to be a minister. Here's what he wrote about me:

"His name is Darcy Fast and you'd better believe it. He is pitching baseball today because he would rather be a preacher than rich and he could become a problem for the people who run NAIA District 2 sports.

Darcy was so fast as a schoolboy pitcher in Washington that he had professional scouts on the doorstep of his father's Church of God parsonage. Some, they say, were bearing alms of promise in figures up to $20,000 for his autograph on a contract.

But Darcy Fast was more interested in the ministry and the bonus that calling promises AFTER his contract ends. Warner Pacific College in Portland offered the church affiliation of his religious background and acquired his pitching services for his name on a standard registration form.

While he is working toward ordination, Fast is converting sundry sinners with his fastball. Lewis & Clark's Pioneers, for instance, got the message in a five-inning informal workout recently. Darcy worked the distance, gave up just two hits and no runs and fanned eight.

Pioneer Coach Fred Wilson was ready to buy the scout's appraisal after that sermon on the mound. "Fast," he agreed, "is fast. I think he throws a slider and I know he has a curveball and good control. He's the real article."

The fact that he could handle a fairly formidable Pioneer club, which has since split with Linfield in an early-season doubleheader, indicates Fast will be little much for the likes of those on Warner Pacific's schedule. In other words, between Darcy and a few days of rain, the team could erect the kind of record that would qualify it for NAIA district playoff consideration."

When I read the article, I thought, *"I have no intention of being a minister. Now, everyone who reads this article, including the scouts, will probably dismiss any thought of me playing professional baseball."*

During my sophomore year, I was pitching against the University of Puget Sound in a non-conference game in Tacoma, Washington when I noticed there were some major league scouts watching the game. I pitched six innings, struck out 11, and didn't give up any runs. I also hit a home run and I began to wonder if I was wrong about my chances of playing professional baseball. After the game, a scout from the Pittsburgh Pirates asked me if I would come to a tryout in Portland. I went to the try-out and pitched against some of the top high school and college players in the area. I didn't give up a single hit—it felt pretty good frustrating those batters.

More scouts, to my amazement, started attending my games. One told me that I was eligible for the Special Phase of the baseball draft in June, which was for players who had been previously drafted but didn't sign. Several scouts had the same question: would I consider signing if I was drafted again, or would I stay in college?

It was a difficult question. I knew I wanted to complete my education, and if playing ball meant jeopardizing that, I wouldn't sign. Staying in college was also important because I didn't want to enter the military draft. The Vietnam War was at its peak then, and I'd known guys from my high school who'd gone over there and returned in body bags. It was a terrible war, and I knew if I went to Vietnam, I probably wouldn't be coming back.

I decided to see if I could work out a compromise with the teams that were interested in me. I told the scouts that I would sign a professional contract *only* if I was allowed to stay in school—I would play ball during the summer. I also said that I'd have to fulfill my military obligation once I graduated and hoped to join the National Guard or Army Reserves.

I let myself start to get excited about playing professional baseball again, though I didn't know what was going to happen. I was still enrolled at Warner Pacific and the Vietnam War was hanging over my head. I wasn't sure how it all was going to work out.

The war itself was very controversial, of course, as everyone who lived through it remembers. It seemed like there were protests every week on college campuses, and many people felt it was a needless war. I didn't understand enough about it back then to know whether we should have been over there or not. There are men my age today who served in Vietnam and were not treated with much respect. When they got back to the United States, protesters threw eggs at some of them when they got off the airplane. Even today, I think very few people appreciate the service performed by the men and women who served in Vietnam, and that isn't right.

I was lucky to be protected from it. I was still in college, and as long as I continued to make progress toward graduation, I didn't have to worry about the draft. Nevertheless, it was on everyone's mind. I remember during freshman orientation, the Dean of Students stood in front of our class and told all the male students that that if we didn't finish in the upper third of our class, we could lose our student deferment. My grades shot right up after that.

I had three goals: stay in college, play professional baseball, and stay out of the military.

E. Joe Gilliam

While I was at Warner Pacific College, I met some amazing people, but the man who had influenced me most at that time was the new college president after Dr. Lewis Gough resigned. His name was E. Joe Gilliam.

Dr. Gilliam served as the president of Warner Pacific for ten years and did a great deal to advance the college during his time there. As a former pastor and author, he was an outstanding story teller and speaker. When he spoke you just wanted to listen—his tall stature and piercing brown eyes added to his intensity. Later, he convinced then-president Gerald Ford to come and speak at the college. Dr. Gilliam became the college president during some lean financial times, and yet through his leadership alone was able to raise the school to a new level of prestige. He had the ability to make people feel like they were the most important person in the world. He certainly made me feel that way.

Dr. Gilliam became a good friend, but, more importantly, he became my mentor, and someone I wanted to emulate. The President's House was close to my dormitory, so I would see him and his children walking their cocker spaniel, "Lovie," in the evenings. We often spoke together about his vision for the college and about my future. I always respected his opinion and he gave me good advice. Years later he asked me to become Vice-President for Advancement at the college, a position I had a difficult time turning down.

Something was brewing in the back of my mind back then, though I wasn't able to understand or articulate it. There were two things I could see myself doing in life that conflicted with each other: my dream of playing professional baseball, and the hazier idea (one that took years for me to understand) of becoming a minister.

I felt as if God had given me the natural tools to be a good baseball player. Yes, I had to work at it like everyone else, but I had a gift and I knew he'd given it to me for a reason. But I wasn't sure what that was, and I often felt confused about my future. For the first time in my life, I felt like I was searching for a deeper purpose. But I never told anyone about it. I internalized the conflict, largely because I didn't want to admit to anybody that going into the ministry was even a possibility. Mostly, I didn't want to admit it out loud—doing that would have made it real. I didn't even talk to JoAnn about it. Years later, when I went into the ministry, JoAnn wasn't that surprised. When people asked her about it she'd say, *"I married a professional baseball player, but if he wants to become a minister, I will support him in what he wants to do."*

I didn't think I'd accept a calling into the ministry, mainly because I felt I'd have to give up too much. What I didn't realize then, and what took many years to learn, is that I had to set aside my own desires to find something better. And at that time, I didn't want to do that: I wanted to be a baseball player, and giving that up was too much. I wanted to be successful. I wanted to make good money. I wanted to become a great pitcher, and I knew that if I went into the ministry, I wouldn't have the fame, money, notoriety, or any of the things that went along with being a major leaguer.

On the other hand, when I observed Dr. Gilliam, I thought, "Man alive! He's influencing so many student's lives." He kept me interested in college and fascinated me with his life of Christian service. He knew about my potential career in professional baseball, and he could see I was struggling with the decision. One day he asked me to have lunch with him. When we sat down, he looked at me with those dark brown eyes of his, and he said, *"Darcy, you'll never know if a professional baseball career is God's purpose for your life until you try it. God needs people in every walk of life, and you could have a great influence on people as a professional athlete."* That stuck with me and it made sense. He'd been reading my mind, and I began to feel better about my pursuit of playing baseball.

The day I signed my first contract, I knew *exactly* what I wanted to do.

The Cubs

George Freese was a scout for the Chicago Cubs. He had short, salt-and-pepper hair, powerful hands, and was a man of few words. He'd played fourteen years of professional baseball, including time with the Pittsburgh Pirates, Detroit Tigers and Chicago Cubs. His brother, Gene Freese, played with the Hawaii Islanders for a year while I was playing in the Pacific Coast League. George was a highly respected scout and manager at the time, and when I learned that he was scouting me, I became pretty excited. He told me that the Cubs had been watching me for some time. Not just during college, in fact, but as far back as high school. I thought it was amazing that they'd even heard of me, considering where I was playing ball. That helped me to see that I didn't have to play for a big school to become a major leaguer. Teams were concerned about potential—I could have been pitching on planet Mars, for all they cared. If I could get batters out, they'd want me.

George came down to our house in Lacey and talked to Dad and me about signing a contract after I had been drafted by the Cubs. He said that the Cubs were willing to let me stay in college if I signed, which was exactly what I wanted to hear. I signed the contract and I got that old feeling back—I was going to make it to the major leagues and fulfill my childhood dream.

And so it happened again. In June of 1967, my sophomore year, the Chicago Cubs drafted me in the sixth round. They wanted me to pitch, although I didn't much care what position they wanted me to play. I would have been happy to be a bat boy if it meant I'd get a chance to get to the major leagues. They knew I could hit, anyway, and I figured I'd get to do a little of both.

I felt pretty good about myself after that, and it was great to get a telegram directly from John Holland, the General Manager of the Cubs, congratulating me. The Cubs signed me to my first professional contract, and included a few special provisions:

"In addition to the salary stated in this contract, if and when approved by the National Association, the Caldwell Baseball Club agrees to pay the sum of $xxxxx payable as follows: $xxxxx upon approval of the contract; and $xxxxx on June 1, 1968. B) Player is to participate in the Professional Baseball College Scholarship Plan, copy of which is being furnished him in connection with this contract. The club agrees to pay authorized college expenses to a maximum of $xxxxx per semester for each of four semesters. C) At the close of the 1967 season the above signed player will receive transportation to the home address indicated on this contract: the mode of travel and route to be taken will be determined by the club."

That bonus was more money than I'd ever seen in my life, but I was even more impressed with the club's decision to pay for the rest of my college education. That showed me they really wanted me.

I was a happy guy and I was excited to begin playing professional baseball. Shortly afterwards, I signed a contract with Topps Baseball Cards & Bazooka Bubble Gum. Not before long, a huge box came to our house while I was living in Lacey with my folks. It was full of Bazooka Bubble Gum and baseball cards—it had every kind of gum that you could think of. We had a fun time dumping the contents of the box out on the floor right there in the living room and going through all the cards. It was like being a kid again. In fact, we got so excited that I lost the check from Topps and I had to have them send me another one.

I felt satisfied knowing that I was beginning a new part of my life, and that my new beginning was the very thing I'd been dreaming about. It was the bubble gum that made me feel like I'd really made it.

Chapter 4

Getting Started

My first season of professional baseball started in Caldwell, Idaho, playing for the Caldwell Cubs in the Pioneer League. When I reported to the team, Gary Nicholson picked me up at the Boise airport and drove me back to the old Caldwell Hotel in a green Ford station wagon. It was about a thirty minute drive. Gary had been the Cubs trainer for the past three years while finishing up his degree at the College of Idaho. As we drove back, we talked a lot about what it was going to be like playing for George Freese and the Chicago Cubs organization. I found out that Gary was very informative, and he gave me some good advice. I remember him telling me that George was particularly impressed with players that worked hard and came ready to play. That was good to know.

We played our home games in a small, well-kept field called Simplot Stadium, which was named after the owner, George Simplot, the Idaho potato magnate. Pat O'Connor was the general manager of the team, and the head grounds keeper—a rare combination. The stock yard was behind the outfield fence, and I can remember hearing the cattle and smelling their aroma they during many night games. Sometimes it could really get to you.

The Pioneer League, which still exists today, is a rookie league made up mainly of first-year ballplayers right out of high school and college. That means most players have shown promise somewhere, but are pretty raw, and are playing in their first ever professional league. The rookie league season is much shorter than other leagues, and runs only from June through August in a schedule of 66 games. The Pioneer League started in 1939 with six teams in Idaho and Utah, and then expanded into Montana about ten years later. There have been about sixty different teams in the league, representing a wide range of major league clubs, but when I played there were four teams: the Caldwell Cubs, the Odgen Dodgers, the Idaho Falls Angels and the Salt Lake City Giants. The league currently has eight teams.

George Freese, who was about 40 at the time, was also the scout who signed me a few weeks before I reported to the team. George had a reputation as an excellent manager and had led the Treasure Valley Cubs to two pennants and two second place finishes—a testament to his ability to work with first-year players. Once when we were playing the Ogden Dodgers in Utah, my roommate Terry Hughes and I got the not-so-bright idea of playing a practical joke on a few players. We left a message and told them the skipper wanted to have a meeting at 11:00 p.m. in the hotel lobby. We'd lost a couple games and so it probably sounded plausible. We thought it was pretty funny and imagined them shaking in their boots, wondering what old George had up his sleeve.

So these guys piled out of their rooms at eleven at night and went to the lobby. Of course, George wasn't there and after a while they got to wondering what was going on. After milling around, everyone just went back to bed. The next day we went out to the ballpark and before the game started George talked to the team in the clubhouse. He did *not* think our joke was funny.

He said, *"I don't know who on this team decided to call some of you last night about a team meeting, but if I don't find out in the next fifteen minutes I can guarantee you there's going be some people here on this ball team that's going to wish they were not on this ball team!"* He stared at us a while, then he said, *"If the guys who made those calls want to step forward right now, I'll take care of them individually. Otherwise, I'll just take care of the whole team."* No one knew what he meant, exactly, but we were young and scared.

We felt pretty stupid, but we didn't want everyone else to get in trouble. Terry and I stepped forward. *"Coach, it was us."*

He said, *"OK. I'll take care of you guys later."*

After that day's game, he chewed us out, but I learned that his bark was a lot worse than his bite. He told us that what we'd done was unprofessional. *"Don't try that when you get further up in base-ball,"* he said. *"Or you'll get yourself in a lot of trouble."* We learned quickly not to mess around with George, and that it was in our best interest to take the game more seriously. I was glad Terry was in on the prank because I knew they weren't going to do anything to their number one draft choice.

Mr. Freese told us he thought our team looked better than the 1966 club that came in second in the Pioneer League. "We've got more speed this year," he told the papers, "and it looks like we're going to have more power." The power hitters on the team were Roy Hutchinson, a classy third baseman from the University of Kentucky, and Enrico Rosendo, a hard hitting first baseman from Puerto Rico, plus my roommate Terry Hughes, who was the second player selected in the major league draft who previously played shortstop at Spartanburg High School in South Carolina.

George also liked the pitching staff. "Our pitching seems to be a bit better than it was at this time last year. We have some real fast ones, more than we started with in '66, and they look like they'll be tough to beat when the season starts next Thursday."

George named me the starting pitcher in the opening game of the season, but he said that I wouldn't pitch more than five innings. "None of the pitchers are ready to try that yet," he said. It was still a great honor. I'll never forget the day we played the Idaho Falls Angels. It was my first professional game and I wanted to make a good impression, but I had the jitters right from the start. After the players were introduced from both teams, I came out from the bullpen where I had been warming up for about 20 minutes and went directly to the mound. Just as I left, Mel Wright, our pitching coach who had been working me, told me to relax and have a good game. He said, "You've got good stuff. Go out and use it in the game." I appreciated the encouragement, but it still didn't help my nerves. I threw a few more pitches to Tom Whelan, our catcher from San Diego, and then he came out to the mound and we went over the signs—nothing complicated; just the basics. One finger for a fastball, two for a curve ball, three for a slider, four for a change-up. I told him quickly before the first batter came to the plate that I wanted to stay with my fastball and curveball as much as possible. I had more confidence in those two pitches. I thought the jitters would go away after I faced the first batter, but I walked him and now I was more nervous. He then managed to steal second base, and if it wasn't for a great double play that got me out the first inning, I doubt whether my nervousness would have left me.

The game started at eight p.m. at Simplot Stadium. There was a lot of buildup in the local papers. The Caldwell News-Tribune said, "Lefthander Darcy Fast will take the mound tonight in starting the Caldwell Cubs on their quest of a third Pioneer League baseball pennant in four years." They also singled out Terry: "Hughes was the nation's No. 2 choice in the recent major league draft and signed for a sizable bonus, with only Atlanta's Ron Blomberg picked ahead of him by the Yankees." There was a lot of pressure on all of us, but more on Terry because he'd been picked so high in the draft. The papers were calling me one of the top prospects in the Cubs organization, though I didn't feel that way. The other guys on the team came from some of the major schools around the country, while I'd come from the tiny Warner Pacific College. It was intimidating, and I had to convince myself that I could compete against All-Americans who had played at Arizona State, USC, UCLA and other schools all over the country. It took a while to make that adjustment, but I finally realized that the other guys put their uniforms on the same way I did: one leg at a time. When we took the field, I saw that I could compete with them.

Mr. Freese planned to spread out our playing time throughout the season in order to give everyone a fair chance to show what they could do. "We want to win," he said that year. "I'm probably the hardest loser there is, but the idea is to develop players. I won't have one set lineup, even in a winning streak, as everyone will get a chance to play. A pitcher with a 15-0 lead probably won't get the opportunity to finish the game." Strangely, later in the year, I *did* complete a game with exactly that margin.

There were only about 1,500 people in the stands for the opening game, but I still had the jitters and couldn't get in the zone like I usually did. Still, I pitched pretty well and didn't give up a hit until the fifth inning, when I lost my concentration. I walked a couple of guys to start the frame, and after an error, gave up a hit and a fielder's choice, and we fell behind 2-1. George came out of the dugout, patted me on the back and took the ball. He put Charley Hunt in after that, and used two other guys to get through the rest of the game. Our leftfielder Jeff Rude had a great game, collecting three hits, including a triple in the fifth that drove in a couple of runs. We scored three in the eighth on three hits—the Angels also threw the ball around a little, which was something George had warned us about. We won 6-2 and I pitched 4 1/3 innings, which wasn't horrible for my first game. I knew that I still had a long way to go, and that I really hadn't proved anything to myself that night.

In the papers the next day, George said, *"Fast ran into a streak of wildness in that inning, so we put Hunt into pitch. Everything's okay now with the first game under our belts. The first game is always the hardest, as everyone's on edge waiting to play after ten to twelve days of practice."* The whole team was a little tight, but that game really loosened us up. "It was a good game for us," George said, "although both sides had some errors and mental mistakes. But the basic fundamentals will win games for us." In the first inning, our left fielder Jeff Rude had thrown out a base runner at third who'd been trying to tag from second. Those were the type of fundamental plays George stressed to us all the time.

I went into a little slump after that first game, and lost my next two starts. I wasn't used to losing, and it was starting to bother me. One of those games was against the Odgen Dodgers. It was insurance night in Simplot Stadium, and Idaho Governor Don Samuelson was there to see the game. I struck out the side twice during the game, but I gave up home runs in the third and fourth innings. I left the game in the eighth and was upset with myself because I didn't finish it. George Freeze said later that "we wasted good pitching by Darcy Fast, and we didn't get the clutch hits with men on base," but I knew if I would have pitched better in the later innings we would have won the game. I could see that the players at this level were a lot better than the players I had competed against during college and semi-pro baseball—these guys were the all-stars from their high

73

school and college teams. I couldn't figure out why I wasn't putting it together.

Fred Martin

In my first three weeks of rookie ball, the team brought in Fred Martin to help the pitchers undo all the bad things we'd learned over the years. Fred was tall and lanky, and he knew more about pitching than anyone I'd ever talked to. His pro career had lasted over twenty-four years—he'd still been an active relief pitcher with the Houston Astros when he was 44. Fred was known as a particularly intelligent instructor who was good at speeding up the development of young prospects.

The first time I met Fred was at Simplot Field in Caldwell. He took me out to the mound on a warm day in June and watched me pitch for about fifteen minutes. That was all the time he needed.

"Darcy, I want you to hold your fastball with the narrow part of the seams," he said, and showed me what he meant. The seams on a baseball help a pitcher spin the ball, naturally, and the faster a ball spins, the more it moves. He changed my curve ball as well. He told me to bear down with my middle finger and thumb when I threw it, rather than with both fingers – the index finger was just along for the ride. The faster a breaking ball spins, the sharper it breaks, and if you don't hold the ball correctly you'll only catch two seams instead of four, which means it won't break as much.

Fred also fine-tuned my pitching mechanics, and this made a tremendous difference. He changed the way I stood on the rubber, and he simplified my delivery. In high school and college, I was a side arm pitcher. Fred showed me how to elevate my arm so I could pitch at about three-quarters. Once I got my elbow up and started holding the ball with the narrow seams, my fastball started tailing away from right-handed hitters and in on left-handed hitters. That was important because I had a lot of natural movement on the ball to begin with, but Fred didn't want the movement to be flat and away. He wanted it to be down and away. I spent a lot of time working on that. Fred also showed me how to hold the ball in the glove and protect it so that the batter couldn't see it until the last possible moment. That way, you didn't give your pitches away. He also explained to me how important it was to mix up my pitches, to throw a curve when they might be expecting a fastball, or to toss in the occasional waste pitch.

Fred not only taught me how to pitch, he taught me how to *think* like a pitcher. I'd come into the dugout after pitching an inning feeling pretty good about myself, and I'd see Fred. He would take his finger and motion over to me. Then he'd review everything that I'd done out there on the mound. He could remember everything and never got too excited. He could tell me what pitch I had thrown to the second batter I faced that inning, and he could also tell me *why* I'd chosen it and why another pitch might have been better. It was like he was reading my mind and getting more out of my playing than I was!

I threw a fast ball, a curve ball, a slider, and then a change-up. Fred taught me to read hitters. If the batter was standing deep in the batter's box, I knew to throw my curve. If he stood up close to the plate I'd probably throw him my fastball. He told me to take control of the game and to not be afraid to pitch inside to the hitters. Even though I had natural ability, I realized that I still had a lot to learn about baseball. I didn't realize just how much that was until I met Fred.

He said, *"Remember to strive for command of your fastball, and then change speeds. If you can do those two things, you'll be successful."*

One day I was pitching against the Salt Lake City Giants, and the batter was up there with a full count. I couldn't decide what pitch to throw in that situation, but I knew I didn't want to walk him. I threw a curve and—bam!—he hit a long home run. When I got out of the inning, Fred came up to me and said, "Darcy, you're thinking too much out there! In that situation always throw your best pitch and your best pitch is your fastball. Stay with it!" I learned from Fred to *"live and die on what you do best."* Fred later showed me how to throw the split-finger fastball, but it took me a long time to gain control of it. Bruce Sutter, the Hall of Famer, gave Fred credit for teaching him the same pitch that enabled him to have such great success as a relief pitcher.

Fred told me that dealing and responding to failure is one of the hardest things for a pitcher to learn. *"Evaluate your pitching after every inning of every game whether you win or lose,"* he said, *"and you will get better and better."* He remained a great friend and teacher throughout my career.

He'd say, *"Darcy, you're going to go somewhere in this organization."* He'd pat me on the shoulder and say, *"When you do, put a good word in for Fred once in a while, will ya?"*

Mustard Seed

I had two roommates that first year at Caldwell: Joe Reyda, and Terry Hughes, who I've mentioned before. Unfortunately, the Cubs figured out not long after they picked Terry that that he just didn't have the range to play short, which was pretty surprising, considering he was the second player selected in the entire country. They moved him to third base later in the season and that was hard for Terry to accept. He was under a lot of pressure and we spent a lot of time talking about it. I was a little older—still just a pup, at 20, but he was 18. This made me feel like something of an elder to him, and I was able to offer some encouragement from time to time. It felt good to be the one helping someone else. I'd tell him simple things, like, *"Terry, you can still make it to the big leagues as a third baseman"* or *"hang in there—you're not going to learn this game in a day."* He actually did make it to the majors, and played a little bit for Chicago, St. Louis and Boston over three seasons.

After hitting under 200 for most of the season, I remember a big game Terry had against the Salt Lake City Giants. It was a game that not only helped him, but helped me, too. Terry got up in the seventh inning with the bases loaded. He hit a grand slam homer and we won the game 12-9. I twisted by right ankle in that inning and was forced to leave the game. If it wouldn't have been for his big hit, I would have lost another game. Terry went 3 for 4 and with that game got his average up over 200. That game really helped his confidence.

Joe Reyda, my other roommate, had already graduated from college and was more mature than me or Terry. He was planning to attend graduate school after the season was over and get a master's degree in economics. We always gave Joe a bad time about his New Jersey accent. I had the feeling that Joe enjoyed playing baseball, but at times he didn't take it too seriously. He was always talking about leaving the game if he didn't get moved up quickly. The three of us rented a two bedroom, furnished basement apartment about a mile from the ball park. We spent a lot of time talking and hanging around together. One day, we couldn't stand our home cooking any longer, so we decided to go into town and have a big steak dinner before the game. We walked to the restaurant and after we got our steaks, Joe was upset over the service and the way his steak was prepared. He wasn't very happy, and everyone there knew it. He became pretty loud and chewed out the waitress, so Terry and I left the restaurant without him. I guess Joe was used to eating in finer restaurants. When we got home that night after the game, we told him if he ever did that again, we'd never go out to eat with him. Most of the time we shared a lot of good laughs and realized that we were living the American dream for every guy who wanted to be a professional baseball player.

After the first month of the season, I was beginning to wonder if I was going to get cut from the team—I was playing poorly. A pro baseball team can release you at anytime and give you the pink slip. There were players coming and going at any given moment. I remember one guy who was signed from the University of Idaho played one week, and that was it—the Cubs released him. I looked at some of the players being released and thought, *"Wow, those guys are better than me!"* Players were constantly being evaluated, and reports were sent to the big club after every game. At this point I was 0 and 2. I'd pitched in three games and I really hadn't shown them much, so I thought I could be sent home any day. I came back to our apartment one night after a game, feeling really down on myself and began thinking and praying about my career. I thought, *"God, why'd you put me in this position if I'm not going to succeed?"* I was kneeling by a sofa and happened to reach under it. To my surprise, I pulled out a little plastic disc about the size of a quarter that had been stuck under the cushions. It was part of a key chain and on one side it had an advertisement for a car— *"Buick - Car of the Year."* On the other side it had a mustard seed. The mustard seed is the world's smallest seed, but when fully developed, it is one of the largest plants in the world. I looked at the mustard seed in the clear plastic, wondering where it came from. Around the seed there was the scripture verse: *"If you have faith as a grain of mustard seed, nothing shall be impossible to you."*

Baseball players are awfully superstitious, and I was no exception, but that little disc represented more than superstition. It represented a promise from God. I believe He gave me that promise when I needed it the most. I took that little disc and kept it for years in my back pocket while I pitched. God had put me in Caldwell for a purpose, and he'd given me both the ability to play professional baseball and the drive to succeed at it, but now it was up to me to have faith in myself and in Him. I started to feel like things would work out and I began to have a new confidence. That was the turning point in my career. From that point on I began to do very well. My first win as a pro came in my fourth start against the Salt Lake City Giants and I started averaging about nine or ten strikeouts a game, leading the league in that category. I also pitched a number of shut outs. As the season progressed, my confidence grew and I really began to blossom as a player. I was even selected to the All-Star team along with my teammates Randy Bobb, Jerry Bongiovanni, Tom Whelan and Tom Krawczyk.

August 12th, 1967 was a hot day in Caldwell and the team was in second place. We needed every win we could get because we were chasing the first place Odgen Dodgers in the standings. I was scheduled to face the Idaho Falls Angels, and I felt pretty good about my chances. I'd been pitching well lately, and we'd already beaten them three games in a row. My arm felt pretty loose warming up, but I had no idea I'd be as dominant as I was that night. The second I took the mound, however, strikeouts started piling up. And they kept coming.

In the end, we crushed them 15-0. I pitched a complete game, struck out fourteen, and scattered seven hits without giving up a run. That's a healthy pitching line, I thought, and Coach Freese said in the papers the next day, *"Darcy pitched a wonderful game. He had real good stuff, moving all the time, and good control. It was quite a performance."* That's when I really began to feel like I could take my pitching to the next level.

My family was excited, too, and when I told them how well I'd done, my father said, *"We want the best for you and we're glad that you're playing so well."*

I remember calling JoAnn once, and after a long talk, I said, *"Maybe someday we'll share all this together."* After all, it was kind of lonely in Caldwell, Idaho. The minor leagues are tough that way. The team would get on a bus and travel eight to twelve hours — sometimes all night — and arrive with just enough time to check into a motel and get to the ballpark. Guys would play cards, read the newspaper or a magazine, strum a guitar, or listen to a transistor radio. I'd try to get comfortable for those long rides. Sometimes I'd climb up in the luggage rack so I could stretch out a little. It was a bus league, so all the teams were in the same boat. The players received only $500 a month, plus a few dollars every day for meals. The team paid for lodging, and we usually didn't eat the best food around — greasy hamburgers and fries, or watery oatmeal. It got pretty tiring. I knew one thing for certain: I wanted to get promoted out of the Pioneer league.

The Ogden Dodgers (the eventual league champions) were the best team we played that year. They were managed by Tommy Lasorda, who was someone I admired. Lasorda had pitched in Canada (he's in the Canadian Hall of Fame) and some in the majors, before he scouted for the Dodgers for about four years. 1967 was only his second year managing, though he must have been a natural—he managed the Ogden Dodgers just three years before the Dodgers promoted him to manage their Triple-A team in Spokane. He made it to the majors in 1973 as a third base coach, and he became the big club's manager when Hall of Famer Walter Alston retired. He'd won five minor league pennants before hitting the majors, and then he immediately led the Dodgers to back-to-back National League championships in 1977 and 78. His Dodgers also won the World Series twice, in 1981 and in 1988. They were tremendous underdogs in 1988. Kirk Gibson hit one of the most famous home runs in World Series history in the opener of that series, and the Dodgers went on to stun the Oakland A's. Lasorda made it to the Hall of Fame as a manager in 1997.

I remember the special relationship he seemed to have with his ballplayers. He was always known as a player's manger—he looked out for the interests of his ballplayers first. We were playing in Ogden and he was eating breakfast with his team. Usually players eat by themselves, and managers and coaches eat together. But when I got down to the lobby that morning and saw Tommy eating with so many of his players, I was amazed. He was laughing with them and telling stories and they were having a great time together. I walked by their table and he said, *"Hey Darcy, how's it going?"*

"It's going great!" I said. I was surprised he even knew me, but I found out later that Tommy Lasorda remembered every ballplayer who ever played for him, as well as most of the ones his teams played against. He was a great guy and I always had fun talking with him. He said, *"There are three types of baseball players: those who make it happen, those who watch it happen, and those who wonder what happens."*

Tommy Lasorda was just another struggling minor league manager in 1967. I'm sure like the rest of us he wanted to get out the Pioneer League, too. I had one of my stronger performances against his team down the stretch, when every game counted. It was August 25th, 1967: it was a cool night, and I was excited to pitch against the Dodgers because I was pitching well. I expected to beat them. I also wanted Lasorda to remember me. We were six games behind the Dodgers at that point, and though it wasn't likely we'd catch them in the standings, it was still possible. George Freese said, *"The mathematical chance is still there for us. The way I figure, we need a series sweep against Odgen, since they play at home next week against the cellar club while we're on the road at Idaho Falls."*

The game started slowly, with neither team scoring in the first two innings. In the third inning, our left fielder, Johnny Johnson, led off with a solo shot over the left field wall that traveled about 350 feet. That loosened everyone up, and the bats really started rolling in the fourth and fifth. In the fourth, John Lung, our All-American third baseman from UCLA, led off with a double. We got three straight singles before Johnny Johnson, who was having a strong game, doubled. We tacked on three more in the fifth and soon the route was on.

Meanwhile, I was dominating. I struck out nine, walked one, and gave up only two singles. For a while I felt as if I was just toying with the Dodger hitters. I went with my fastball about sixty percent of the time, and used my curve and change up for the other forty percent. It was the closest I would ever come to pitching a perfect game as a professional. My strikeouts boosted my league-leading total to 129, and I lowered my earned run average to 3.03. It was an odd game in some ways, too, because the Dodgers hit only two fly balls into the outfield (besides the two singles) and our first baseman and catcher, Tom Whelan and Randy Bobb respectively, accounted for twenty-one of the twenty-seven putouts: Tom with 11, Randy with 10. The final score was 7-0.

Tacoma

On one of the last two days of the season, George Freese told me the Cubs were calling me up to Tacoma, which was the Triple-A team in the Pacific Coast league for the Chicago Cubs. I thought they were just sending me there because it was close to home.

I asked George, *"They want me to throw batting practice up there, right?"*

He said, *"No, they want you to pitch against the Hawaii Islanders."*

"Are you kidding me?" I asked. Only one player on the whole team had been promoted that season, and he had only been called up to class A ball in Lodi, California. Suddenly, I was going from the rookie league, which isn't even class A ball, to Triple-A. I really couldn't fathom it. To me, Triple A was not that much different from the major leagues. There were a handful of former major leaguers on the teams at that level, plus guys on rehab assignments. It meant I was going to get a chance to play with the best and most promising players in the organization. I was excited, too, because Tacoma is only about twenty minutes from my hometown, and I was sure that my high school coaches and other friends would come out to watch me pitch.

Pitching in Cheney Stadium and in the Pacific Coast League was going to be a great experience. I had watched the Tacoma Giants play at Cheney many times while in school and often thought it would great pitching there. Cheney Stadium was built in 1960 by Ben Cheney, the lumber baron who figured out that by standardizing lumber in eight-foot lengths, he could save and make lots of money. The San Francisco Giants committed to moving their Triple-A Phoenix team to Tacoma in 1959, provided that Tacoma would construct a stadium by April, 1960. The Giants remained in Tacoma until 1966, when the Chicago Cubs brought their top affiliate to Tacoma. The whole area could now enjoy professional baseball, because at that time, we didn't have any major league teams in the Pacific Northwest.

The Pacific Coast League has had a long tradition on the West Coast. In the early 20th century, it developed into one of the premier regional baseball leagues. With no Major League Baseball team existing west of St. Louis, the PCL was unrivaled as the best in West Coast baseball. It was never recognized as a true major league, but the quality of play was considered very high. Most of the players at that time came from the West Coast, and the PCL produced a number of outstanding players, including future major-league stars Joe DiMaggio, Ted Williams, Tony Lazzeri, Earl Averill and Ernie Lombardi. While many PCL stars went on to play in the major leagues, teams in the league were often so successful that they could offer competitive salaries to avoid being outbid for their star's services. In 1952, the PCL became the only minor league in history to be given the "open" classification, a step above the AAA level.

I arrived at Cheney Stadium two days early so I would have the opportunity to get to know some of the players and get a feel for what a Triple-A team was like. When I walked into the clubhouse for the first time, I met most of the players as they were getting ready for the game. I noticed right away that they were a little older and more mature than at Caldwell. You could tell they had been around baseball for a longer time, as they had a certain swagger and confidence about them. The clubhouse was small, but very nice—the lockers were large, and the food was always available. The clubhouse manager and clubhouse boys were polishing shoes and getting the uniforms and equipment ready for that night's game. I tried to act relaxed around them, but I really felt like a rookie and I wasn't sure I was ready to play Triple-A baseball. It didn't take long before they started joking around with me, which let me relax a little.

My new manager, Whitey Lockman, called me into his office and told me I'd be pitching in two days—on Saturday night. He said I would be charting pitches the night before I pitched, and that I should sit next to the charting pitcher at tonight's game, who would show me what to do. I had never heard of this before, but when I saw how much charting a game helped prepare you, I was eager to do it.

I found out later that Whitey Lockman had kept the Tacoma Cubs in the thick of the Pacific Coast League pennant race for most of the year and that he always had a strong desire to win. He was tall, lanky, and got right to the point when he talked to you. Whitey gained the distinction of being one of the few players to make it in Triple A baseball at age 16, and the majors at age 18. Whitey broke into the major leagues in 1945 with the New York Giants. After military service, he went on to star in the outfield, and later at first base for the Giants, part of the time while under Manager Leo Durocher. He played with the Giants in 1951 when they won the National League pennant in the historic playoff against the Dodgers. He played in the 1951 and '54 World Series, and he was the National League All-Star first baseman in 1952. I knew my new skipper had exceptional baseball skills and was extremely knowledgeable about the game.

The catcher for my first game at Tacoma was John Boccabella. He was a strong, hard-nosed player with plenty of experience, and he had a bright future ahead with the Cubs. John and I went over some of the signs and I told him what kinds of pitches I threw. He'd never seen me pitch before, of course, so he spent extra time with me warming me up before the game. I felt nervous, but confident, and tried to keep in mind everything Fred Martin had taught me.

Not long before the game, the clubhouse manager told me the only uniform they had for me was one that Dick Radatz had worn. Dick Radatz's nickname was "The Monster," because he was a huge guy. He'd been a dominating closer in the bigs leagues for the Red Sox (1962-66), Indians (1966-67), Cubs (1967), and later pitched for the Tigers (1969) and the Expos (1969). Radatz led the American League in saves (24), games (62), and relief wins (9) in 1962, his rookie season with the Red Sox, and he was named Fireman of the Year by The Sporting News. In 1963, he saved 25 games and went 15-6 with a 1.97 ERA. He was the first pitcher in history to have back to back 20-save seasons. He made the All-Star team that year, where he made a name for himself by striking out Duke Snider, Willie Mays, and Willie McCovey. He earned his second Fireman of the Year award in 1964 when he won 16 games with a 2.29 ERA and led the league with 29 saves. He once struck out 181 batters in a season, which is the most by a reliever, even to this day. He *was* a monster. But Radatz started to have arm troubles and in 65 went 9-11 and had an ERA near 4.0. After surgery, Radatz was never the same, which is why he bounced around from team to team. He was in Tacoma that year trying to recover his form. Later, he was selected to the Boston Red Sox Hall of Fame (1997). He died in March 2005 after falling down a flight of stairs at his home.

Back in 1967, I was a pretty big guy myself. I was 6'3" and weighed about 195 lbs, but Radatz was just plain bigger. He was 6'5" and weighed about 240, so his uniform did not fit me. Not even close. It was very baggy and uncomfortable, but there was nothing I could do about it. Usually teams tailor uniforms for their players, but it was right at the end of the season and it was too late for that. I felt a little ridiculous, but I was happy to get the chance to pitch in a Triple- A game. As it turned out, the uniform didn't affect my performance.

The Hawaii Islanders were the Triple A team for the Washington Senators and one of the best hitting teams in the league. They were managed by Wayne Terwilliger, affectionately known as "Twig." In 2005, Twig completed his 57th season in professional baseball and managed the Fort Worth Cats to the championship of the independent Central League. He was named Manager of the Year and then announced his retirement. At 80, he was the oldest active manager in baseball, and the only man besides Connie Mack to manage after turning 80. Twig has been in uniform for more than 7,000 professional games as a player, coach, and manager. At a welcome party for his team during the beginning of the Islander's season, Twig said, "Who says you can't win 'em all?" He told the crowd he'd always considered the statement's alternative to be negative and a cop-out. After his team won five straight, spectators, too, were saying, "Who says you can't win 'em all?" However, they lost the next game, and quite a few more after that.

Key players on the Hawaii Islanders were Dick Bosman, who made use of the sinker and the "slurve," and who (as a Senator) a few years later would lead the American League with a 2.19 ERA, and outfield "Toothpick" Willie Kirkland, whose big bat resulted in a lot of strikeouts, but also a lot of home runs. Kirkland led the PCL that year in home runs (34) and RBI's (97). I was warned not to give him anything good to hit.

As I walked out to the mound that evening from the bullpen I noticed how beautiful Cheney Stadium looked, and how manicured the infield was before the start of the game. It was a warm evening, and I remember Boccabella's last words to me were, "throw strikes and stay ahead of the hitters." He said, *"they'll be taking a lot of pitches at first to see what you've got."* I was pretty excited when they introduced me as the starting pitcher for the Tacoma Cubs just before they played the Star-Spangled Banner. I turned to center field and tried to focus on what I was going to throw the first batter, but there were too many butterflies. The stands were full of people I knew who were watching me pitch professionally for the first time, and many more were listening to the game on the radio. I just needed to relax and rely on Boccabella's knowledge of the hitters. My job was to pitch whatever he called for and get it over the plate.

The first inning, I struck out the first three batters I faced. Just like Boccabella said, they were looking at a lot of pitches. The second inning, Willie Kirkland led off. I remembered from charting pitches the night before that I had to keep the ball away from him. He was a dead fastball hitter and so I started him off with an off-speed curve ball and he let it go by for strike one. I was a little surprised that Boccabela called for the same pitch because you usually throw your off-speed pitches when you're behind in the count. I threw it again though, and he did the same thing—let it go by for strike two. I was pretty sure now that he would have me waste a fastball outside and that's exactly what I did. With the count now at 2 strikes and 1 ball, I threw a hard breaking pitch and he struck out. That was a big out, and I finally began to relax! The next two batters struck out, and in two innings, I now had six strike outs. I was surprised, but I kept walking off the mound as if I knew what I was doing. Our hitting was great in the early innings, too. Boccabella hit a pair of monumental home runs, the first one coming in the first inning with Marv Breeding aboard, and the next one in the third with the bases empty. His third-inning shot was a line drive which carried over the right-centerfield fence by a comfortable margin at the 410 mark and may have been the longest hit ever at Cheney Stadium. I remembered what Fred Martin had told me so many times— *"You've got to bear down more when you have a good lead."* The 3-0 lead wasn't enough for me, and I gave up three runs in the fourth on three singles, two walks, and a wild pitch. The Islanders rallied to pull even. I had 13 strikeouts at the end of six and finished with 15. I didn't even know it until I pitched two more innings and came out in the 8th to a huge applause. The announcer said, *"Tacoma Cubs pitcher Darcy Fast has just tied the Pacific Coast League single game strike-out record with 15 strikeouts."* It was a great thrill! We ended up losing the game, however, in part because of my own throwing error on a swinging bunt in the second inning. The fifteen strikeouts eclipsed Hall of Fame pitcher Juan Marichal's Tacoma strikeout record.

That game was the launching pad for my major league career, and I was brimming with confidence. According to a lot of scouts, I was now a can't-miss major league prospect. Bobby Adams, who was the general manager of the Tacoma Cubs and who had managed the Chicago Cubs, said I was going to be the most exciting thing to happen to Tacoma Cubs baseball since Juan Marichal. He said, *"My only regret is I don't think we'll have him for very long before he'll be in the major leagues."* When I started reading things like that—and believe me, baseball players do read the newspapers—I thought, *"Someone thinks that I'm going to make it."* Still, I also remembered someone telling me, *"Don't believe everything that's written about you."*

Chapter 5

The Call

❖❖

I was very excited about going to spring training in 1968. I'd had a successful, if brief, minor league career already, and I was looking forward to my chance to impress the Cubs organization in Scottsdale, Arizona. Even though I wasn't in the major league camp—I'd signed a minor league contract with the Tacoma Cubs—I was pleased to have a chance at Triple-A again. I thought that if I could impress the coaches there, I'd have a good chance of playing in Chicago that season. I was aware that there were guys on the 40-man major league roster, of course, who would be coming down to take spots on the Triple-A team, so I didn't feel too secure. I knew I was competing against ballplayers that had a lot more experience than I did, but I was having a good spring training and I thought for sure that I would make the Tacoma team.

When spring training started, Bobby Adams, the general manager of the Tacoma Cubs, told the newspapers, "Fast may need additional seasoning, but he may also be ready to step right in and do the same kind of job as certain other pitching phenoms in the organization— youngsters such as Ken Holtzman, who became a regular with the big club after only one full year as a professional."

I appreciated his comments, but once again I reminded myself, "Don't believe everything that's written about you."

Toward the end of spring training, Whitey Lockman, the manager of the Tacoma Cubs, and Bobby Adams told me that the Cubs were assigning me to Lodi, California to play for the Lodi Crushers in the California League, which was Single A. Whitey told me the Cubs thought very highly of me and although I performed well at Triple-A ball during spring training, they still wanted me to get more experience in A ball. Mr. Adams told the newspapers, *"He could come so fast that he'll be back with us in a month. He wanted badly to pitch for the benefit of family and friends from Lacey, and he'd better do so soon, because he's going to be at Wrigley Field before long."* I was disappointed to start the season in Lodi, but I also knew that one good game in Triple-A did not necessarily mean that I was ready to pitch at that level. I resolved to do the best I could at Lodi in the California League and see if I couldn't get called back up. I realized that starting the season at Tacoma would be a big jump in the organization.

The California League is a minor league which operates throughout the state of California. It was classified as a "High-A" league, indicating its status as a Class A league with the highest level of competition within that classification, and it is the fifth step between rookie ball and the major leagues. Most of the players in the league, including those in Lodi, were early-round draftees with either college experience or several years of professional experience. Generally, players do not arrive as this level until their third or fourth year of professional baseball.

A couple of my buddies who played for Lodi were Chris Barkulis and Bruce Carmichael. Barkulis was in his third year as a Crusher. Born in Chicago, where he played high school baseball, he batted .619 in his senior year and in an all-star game at Wrigley Field, he hit two doubles off the wall. He then received a four-year scholarship to Bradley University and signed with the Chicago Cubs two days after he graduated. In his first full year in professional baseball, Chris led the league in hitting at Quincy, Illinois with a .336 average. He was then assigned to Lodi where he hit .285 and rapped 22 homers with 94 runs batted in. Because of a broken ankle, Chris missed his chance of being moved up to Double-A at Dallas-Fort Worth. Chris had a great personality and was a natural leader on the team. Barkulis was good to have in the clubhouse because he kept everyone loose with his jokes.

Bruce Carmichael received a four-year baseball scholarship from Santa Clara after graduating from Stagg High School. Batting lead-off at Santa Clara, Carmichael ripped a .339 average in his junior year and his .310 in his senior year. Carmichael was signed by the Cubs after college and assigned to the Lodi Crushers. He played shortstop and second base, and was batting over .300 with five home runs.

Jim Colburn was one of my best friends in baseball, and we first met in Lodi when he had been sent down from Double-A San Antonio, as he wasn't pitching very well. The Cubs wanted him to get things worked out there. We played together at Lodi and Tacoma and became good friends. When he was assigned to Lodi, he didn't have a place to stay. I invited him to share my apartment until I got married. Jim spent 10 years as a pitcher in the major leagues and currently is the pitching coach for the Pittsburg Pirates. Prior to becoming a pitching coach, Jim served as the Director of Pacific Rim Scouting for the Seattle Mariners for four years (1997-2000). I was talking with him during a time when I watched Tacoma Rainiers games with my family, and he told he was instrumental in the signing of 2000 American League Rookie-of-the-Year Kazuhiro Sasaki, and 2001 A.L. MVP Ichiro Suzuki.

On May 8th, I started the game against the Fresno Giants in Fresno. They were considered to be one of the better teams in the league, and several of their players went on to have major league careers. I was cruising along and throwing nothing but blanks for 8 innings and had a no hitter until the 6th inning. I had fanned 10 batters. Pitching is really mental, and you have to develop a good mental approach to pitching before you can become a good one. At first I didn't realize this—I thought a pitcher was at his best when he throws hard and strikes out a batter. Lew Burdette, a pitcher for the Braves said, "I exploit the greed of all hitters." Satchel Paige once said, "Just take the ball and throw it where you want to. Throw strikes. Home plate don't move." And Warren Spahn once commented, "A pitcher needs two pitches—one they're looking for, and one to cross 'em up. Hitting is timing. Pitching is upsetting timing."

There are times when you're pitching that you get into a groove—when the ball goes right where you want it to. That is the best feeling a pitcher can have. It's like a "runner's high," and when you're in the grove, you believe there isn't a hitter that you can't get out. That's the way I felt that night.

In the first inning Chris Barkulis hit a "slap" shot to left after Bruce Carmichael walked and John Dudek's pop single to left field gave us a 1-0. When I entered the ninth inning, we had a 3-0 lead and things were looking pretty good, but that changed quickly. The Giants' Rafle Robles and Chris Arnold hit back to back singles, and then Bob Fenwick hit a booming double and both runners scored. Now the score was 3-2 and the next batter, Bernie Williams, got the count to 3-2 before the Giants' huge right fielder clubbed a deep shot to left field. Leroy Haynes, our left fielder, raced across the foul line and out of the playing area to make a great catch. It appeared to everyone that Haynes was well off the playing area when he made the grab, but the umpires thought differently and called the batter out. The fans went crazy, and the entire Giants bench emptied and swarmed around the umpires in a moment arguing the call, but the umpires refused to change their decision. I quickly left the mound and went into the club house thinking that if I were off the field, the umpires would stick to their decision. They did, and we won the game. To this day, I believe that Haynes had to be at least 10 feet out of play when he caught the ball, and it was one of the worst calls I've even seen in baseball. Well, everyone gets lucky once in a while.

By June 1st, I had a 6-2 record and was leading the California League in strikeouts—89 in 86 innings pitched—and I began to hope I'd get called up again, either to Double-A ball, which was at San Antonio, Texas or back to Triple-A in Tacoma. However, I wasn't getting any feedback from my manager, Jim Marshall, so I really wasn't sure what would happen. I decided that the best thing I could do was to continue playing good baseball for Lodi.

Jim Marshall was a good communicator and had a great sense of humor. He was an easy guy to play for because he kept the team relaxed and he stood up for his players. During his professional career, he bounced around for five seasons in the big leagues, playing for the Cubs, Mets, Orioles, Giants and Pirates, and was part of the first inter-league trade (without waivers) in baseball history when the Cubs traded him to the Boston Red Sox on November 21, 1959. He was also the starting first baseman in the first National League game ever played by the New York Mets in 1962. Later in his career, he went on to manage the Chicago Cubs (1974-76) and the Oakland Athletics (1979) but never had a winning season, and his terrible A's team lost 108 of 162 games. Marshall also played in Japan from 1963 to 1967. Lodi was his first job as a manager.

Sometimes the seasons in the minors seem like they can go on forever. One evening, we were playing a game and our bullpen catcher took a pitch off his throat while warming up one of our pitchers. He didn't have his facemask on and he was pretty badly hurt. The first base umpire called time out, and everyone jumped up and started charging out of the dugout to see how he was doing. I started charging too, but as I was running out of the dugout I smacked my head on a pipe and knocked myself out. In the meantime, our entire team, including the manager, was down in the bullpen to check on him. When they walked back they found me lying unconscious on the cement floor. They thought it was pretty funny once I came around and they saw I was okay. That's how I got my first (and only) professional nickname. Every player gets a nickname eventually, and from that point on, they called me "Daisy" because the pipe had "dazed me" in the middle of a game. It was the only time in my pro career that I had to go the hospital to get checked out for an injury. It was embarrassing to tell the doctors I hadn't been hit by a ball or a stray bat, but by a low hanging drainpipe.

Marriage

I was given permission to leave the team for three days in late May and flew to Olympia. JoAnn and I were married June 1st. Our wedding was held at the Olympia Lacey Church of God, where my father had been the pastor for eleven years. It was the church I'd grown up in. My high school coaches, Jim Fouts and Archie McCallum, were there, plus one of my favorite teachers, Jim Stuart. It was a large wedding, held on a very rainy day. My father officiated, and my brother Dallas played the organ. JoAnn and I sang to each other, *"Whither Thou Goest I Will Go,"* and we had a beautiful reception afterward. In spite of this sudden immersion in the church, I was not distracted: I still hoped I'd get to play in the major leagues. Seeing my father officiate the wedding and holding it in our old church did nothing to change my mind—the ministry was not something I thought much about. I was too busy playing baseball.

We spent our first night at the Tyee Motor Inn in Olympia. Oddly, I wasn't the only professional athlete in the motel that evening, and not the most famous. Daryl Lamonica, who was a quarterback for the Oakland Raiders, was staying in the hotel, too. At breakfast, we were introduced, and he told me that he had turned down a professional baseball contract with the Chicago Cubs to play football at Norte Dame. In 1967, Lamoinca was traded to the Oakland Raiders and threw for thirty touchdown passes, leading the Oakland Raiders to the American Football League Championship. He wished us the best in our marriage and my career. The next day, we drove back down to Lodi, California. We were driving a Volkswagen beetle at the time, so we had to open most of our gifts during the reception— we couldn't possibly take them all in that little bug. We transported what we could manage, plus a few essentials we needed to set up our apartment, and started the long drive back to California.

That was our honeymoon. We arrived at our little one bedroom apartment in Lodi and set up house. We were there for a little over a week and a half when, one morning, someone knocked on our apartment door. It was Jim Marshall, the manager of the Crushers.

"Can I talk you to?" he said.

"Sure can, Come on in" I replied.

He said, *"I've got some good news for you. You're being called back up."*

I thought he meant that I was going to be called back up to Double-A San Antonio, or maybe even Triple-A Tacoma. Either would have been great to me. Most of the time, players have to go through all three levels of the minors—Single-A to Double-A to Triple-A—so skipping Double-A would have been exciting.

"You'd better pull up a chair," Marshall said. *"I've got even better news than that. You're being called up to the majors."*

I couldn't believe it.

He said, *"I've got an airline ticket for you. You'll be leaving from San Francisco today, and you're going to be meeting the team in Atlanta."*

"I'm not sure I'm ready," I said, holding my breath.

"They're not gonna bring you up there unless they feel you're ready to pitch there."

And just like that, I was heading for the majors. Everything became a whirlwind after that. Jim Collburn and Chris Barkulis helped JoAnn pack up all of our stuff again, and she drove back up to Olympia until she could meet me in Chicago. JoAnn was surprised that things were happening so fast, and though we would be separated for awhile, she was really happy for me. I told her you never know what's going to happen when you're a baseball player, and that we have to be prepared to move at any time.

From that point on everything was a blur. I was on an airplane leaving San Francisco, looking at the ground sliding past, thinking about my future. I got off in Atlanta and went to the Marriot Motor Inn where I was going to meet my team. I arrived late in the evening and was told at the front desk that the Marriot Hotel was filled to capacity. I got my key and went up to my room to get some sleep. From the outside, the room looked like just an ordinary room. When I opened the door, I couldn't believe what I saw—there was a separate foyer, dinning room, conference room, two luxury bathrooms, and two bedrooms—one much larger than the other, and with an official insignia above the bed. After I finished looking around, I called down to the front desk and asked them if they'd made a mistake.

The man at the desk said, *"No,"* Mr. Fast. *"We haven't made a mistake. We don't have any other place to keep you tonight except for the Presidential Suite."* That was my welcome to the big leagues.

The following morning, I met many of the ballplayers in the lobby as the others were eating breakfast in the hotel restaurant. Things were happening very quickly and I was pretty intimidated, so I didn't have a lot of time to talk to any of the players at first—just a lot of handshaking and best wishes. *"Glad you're here,"* they said. *"Good luck."* A bunch of us piled onto the elevator to go up to our rooms, and when I looked around, I was surrounded by guys like Ron Santo, Don Kessinger, and the irrepressible Ernie Banks. The Cubs were in a four game series with the Braves. The first game on Friday, they won 2-1 behind the great pitching of Rich Nye. The team was in 5th place in the National League with a 30-29 record. I had just turned twenty-one, and I couldn't help thinking that I still had a collection of bubblegum cards with the faces of these players on them. It was quite a change from eating hamburgers in Lodi, California. Now I was going to eat steaks with the Chicago Cubs.

The manager of the Cubs that year was Leo Durocher. Durocher, nicknamed *"Leo the Lip,"* had been a light hitting infielder in the majors for the Yankees, Reds, Cardinals and Dodgers, but he made his name as a manager. When he retired in 1973, he ranked fifth all-time among managers with 2,008 wins, and second only to John McGraw in National League history—he ranked ninth all time as recently as 2005. He was something of a troublemaker and liked to argue, sometimes just for its own sake. I remember him rushing out on to the field many times, flipping his cap backwards, and getting right in the umpire's face. He was ejected from more games than any manager in the history of the game, and that record still stands today. Durocher liked tough, gritty players, and he wasn't afraid to chew someone out, especially the young players. One of his favorite all time players was Eddie Stanky, the tough second baseman on his 1951 pennant winning Giants team. Stanky was known for his ability to draw walks—he drew 100 walks in 6 seasons and twice managed to get 140—and for his tough play, distracting batters by jumping up and down behind second. Durocher once said, *"He can't hit, he can't field, he can't run—all he can do is beat you."*

Durocher won his first NL pennant with the Dodgers in 1941, and continued to manage them until 1946, but he had a problem: he liked to gamble. He got into trouble with the league a lot and was constantly being reprimanded by then-commissioner Albert "Happy" Chandler. Durocher was good friends with a few actors—George Raft and Frank Sinatra, for example—and once admitted knowing the notorious gangster, Bugsy Siegel. He also liked to play cards and would get games going with the older guys in the clubhouse, and he was known as a bit of a pool shark. He got into some trouble early in his career for rigging a clubhouse game of craps and bilking one of his own players of some money. He was suspended, in fact, for the entire 1947 season for consorting with gamblers.

But Durocher just wanted to win, and he helped integrate baseball, because he only cared what a player could do for him on the field. He was a big supporter of Jackie Robinson, who was his type of player, and told the team before Robinson joined that he wouldn't tolerate anyone who didn't treat Robinson right. He was quoted as saying, *"I don't care if the guy is yellow or black, or if he has stripes like a (blank) zebra. I'm the manager of this team, and I say he plays."*

Durocher was fired right in the middle of the 1948 season, but was immediately picked up by the New York Giants. He got a little revenge on his old team a few years later. He was the manager of the 1951 NL pennant winning team that made up 13-and-a-half games in 6 weeks. They beat the Dodgers on Bobby Thompson's famous walk-off home run off Ralph Branca, *"The Shot Heard 'Round the World."* Little did Durocher know that his '69 Cubs team would suffer a similar collapse.

Durocher won his only World Series Championship in 1954 when the Giants swept the Cleveland Indians, who had posted an incredible 111-43 record in the regular season. He managed through 1955 and worked as a TV commentator for a few years before working as a coach with the Dodgers, who had moved to Los Angeles. Durocher, always a bit of a publicity hound, appeared on TV in those years, playing himself in episodes of *"The Munsters" and "Mr. Ed."*

Durocher took the reigns of the Cubs in 1966 and managed them until 1972. He sometimes had problems with some of the stars, and nearly got in a fight with Ron Santo one time in the clubhouse. On one occasion, Durocher had lit up Santo for not taking batting practice, Durocher accused him of asking John Holland to have a "Ron Santo Day" because Ernie Banks and Billy Williams had one. Santo charged at Durocher, and they fought until some players quickly broke them up. Durocher lived to regret what happened, and died in Palm Springs, California at the age of 86. He was inducted into the Baseball Hall of Fame in 1994.

Blake Cullin, the traveling secretary for the Cubs, gave me a little brown envelope the day after I arrived. *"This is the money you'll use for eating and while you're on the road,"* he said. *"We want you to remember one thing: when you go out, we want you to tip well, because you're representing the Chicago Cubs now."* There was more money in that little envelope—our per diem—than the entire sum of my last check in the minors.

Rich Nye and I became friends almost immediately after I joined the team. He was one of the National League's top left-handed pitchers in 1967. He invited me to share his apartment with him in Chicago, near Lake Shore Drive and Irving Park, before JoAnn and I found a place of our own. We spent a lot of time talking baseball and eating out together. His 13 victories, 205 innings pitched, 30 starts, 7 complete games and 119 strikeouts were figures topped only by Fergie Jenkins on the Cubs staff. Rich, like other members of the Cubs' young pitching staff, improved as the year went on, winning 4 of his last 5 decisions. When Rich told me that he moved into the Cubs staff after only one year as a pro, I felt better about my chances, since I had spent less than one year in the minors. Rich was selected by the Cubs in the free agent draft of June 1966 from the University of California, where he graduated with a degree in Civil Engineering. He went on to graduate from the Veterinary School at the University of Illinois, and is living in western suburbs of Chicago, where he is considered one of the foremost experts on exotic bird diseases.

I remember eating with him and Joe Niekro at the Old Original Bookbinder's Restaurant when we were playing in Philadelphia. The popular restaurant is located near the Delaware River and was started in the late 1800's. The Chesapeake Bay offered its bounty of oysters, crabs, and clams. That day I got a little taste of the way ballplayers can be treated. When we arrived, there was a line out the door for people waiting to be seated. Rich told us to wait outside for a minute and in short time we were ushered into the dinning room past many people and seated immediately. We ate buttered clams, steak and lobster—I knew I was a major league ballplayer when people starting coming over to our table for autographs.

The afternoon of my first day on the team, we went out to the ballpark in Atlanta and I met Durocher and some of the other coaches on the team. We headed out to the ball park in a chartered bus, and I got my first glimpse of Atlanta Stadium. I had never even been to a major league ballpark before, let alone played in one. When I walked into my first major league clubhouse, the scene startled me. I had just turned 21 with less than a full year of minor league ball behind me, and I had never seen players smoking in a clubhouse. Some players were sitting around their lockers playing cards or reading, and Frank Sinatra was singing *"Chicago—My Kind of Town"* over the speakers. Al Scheuneman, our trainer, was wrapping the ankles of a few players and watching over others in the whirlpool. Yosh Kawano, the equipment manager, was getting the bats and helmets out and taking care of the uniforms. The clubhouse was huge. There were clubhouse boys running around, and Yosh was making sure everyone got everything they needed. When I saw the locker with my name on it, I went over and started to put on my uniform. My shoes were polished, and my warm-up jacket was hanging in the locker—and my shirts were clean and all ready to go. I was amazed that every thing I needed was taken care of before I could ask—this was a lot different than Lodi. A buzz ran through my whole body as I walked from the clubhouse to the ball field, proud just to be wearing the Cubs uniform.

Atlanta Stadium had been constructed in just fifty weeks and opened for the first time in the spring of 1965, although the Braves didn't move there until 1966. It was really nothing special—it was a cookie cutter stadium—and it was known for having a poorly manicured field. In spite of these faults, it was still better than anything I'd ever played on. It seated 52,013 fans, which was huge compared to any other place I'd ever played. Because Atlanta has a fairly high elevation, resting as it does near the foothills of the Appalachian Mountains, it was pretty easy to hit a baseball a long way there. The stadium soon earned the nickname, *"The Launching Pad."* The official name was changed to the Atlanta-Fulton County Stadium in the 70s, and it was finally demolished on August 2, 1997. The Braves were a .500 team in their first few years in Atlanta and were headed for a .500 year in 1968, though they'd go on to win the first ever National League west division crown before being swept by the Miracle Mets for the Pennant in 1969.

The fans there loved Hank Aaron, who was arguably the greatest home run hitter who ever lived. I was excited at the prospect of seeing the slugger, and even more thrilled at the idea that I might get to face him. By the end of the 1973 season, Aaron had hit 713 home runs, which was just one short of Babe Ruth's record. Throughout the winter, he received death threats, because many people didn't want to see a black man break Babe Ruth's record. On April 4, 1974, he hit number 714 in Cincinnati, and on April 8, in front of his adoring home fans, he broke the record. The parking lot for Turner Field, the current Braves' home, now stands where the old building stood with a plaque marking the spot where Aaron's 715th career home run landed.

I was awed, and all the blinking in the world couldn't get the stardust out of my eyes. I was pretty nervous, too, because I knew I was going to be playing with a whole different caliber of ballplayer in the major leagues. I kept thinking, "How in the world can I be ready for this?" The Cubs had traded a left-handed pitcher in the bullpen named Ramon Hernandez. That trade had created an opening for me. The Cubs had 30 wins and 29 losses. The team was in 5th place and 7 games behind the Cardinals. I just hoped I'd be able to help.

Our bullpen coach was Verlon "Rube" Walker. He'd been a catcher, and was probably best known for his ability to work with young players. Rube pulled me aside and told me I was going to be in the bullpen, and that Durocher planned to use me as a relief pitcher. Until then, I had always been a starting pitcher, so I wasn't sure how to even go about preparing to come in for a relief appearance. Starters have a lot more time to warm up.

The night was 80 degrees and cool for Atlanta. Joe Niekro started for the Cubs, and he was opposed by Milt Pappas, who was making his debut for the Braves. Chicago jumped out to a 2-0 lead in the second and could have had more. Ron Santo walked, and then Ernie Banks hit an easy double play ball, but the Braves second baseman dropped the shortstop's throw and both runners were safe. After failing to get a bunt down, Lou Johnson, our right fielder, laced a triple to center field, scoring both Santo and Banks. Adolpho

Philips, the next batter, lifted a fly to medium left, and Johnson raced home on the sacrifice to give the Braves a 3-0 lead. Only Johnson left early! The Braves appealed, and he was called out. That mental error eventually cost us dearly. In the third, Don Kessinger tripled to left center, but neither Glenn Beckert nor Billy Williams, who was in the middle of a slump, managed to bring him in. Deron Johnson hit a two run home run off Niekro in the fourth, and the score stayed the same for the next few innings. Don Kessinger was having a good game and ended with three hits. Joe Torre, the longtime Yankees manager, was the catcher for the Braves, but he was hitless. I spent the entire game in the bullpen, watching and sitting next to the other relief pitchers.

The phone rang in the bullpen in the sixth inning. Rube Walker said, *"Fast, the skipper wants you to warm up."* Walker was a soft-spoken man who was in his eighth year as a member of the Cubs coaching staff. I found out later that he had spent his entire career with the Cubs organization. He caught for 7 different clubs and was originally nicknamed "Little Rube" because of his older brother Al, who'd also earned the nickname "Rube" when he caught for the Cubs.

The score was 2-2 and there were over 27,000 fans screaming and yelling. It was bat day, and there were probably 15,000 kids waving little bats in the stands. I figured they just wanted me to get loose to see me throw—no one on the staff had even seen me pitch, so there was no way I was getting in the game. All the information they had on me was just from the scouting reports, so I just took my time. After about five minutes, Walker approached me again.

"Are you ready?" he said.

"Ready for what?" I replied.

He looked at me like I was crazy. *"Are you ready to go in the ballgame?"*

"Let me throw a little bit more," I said as calmly as I could. I thought there was no way they were going to put me into the game with the score tied on my first day with the team. But I knew he wasn't kidding when Joe Becker, the Cubs' pitching coach, came running toward the bullpen to watch me pitch. Becker became the pitching coach the previous year and had an outstanding record for developing young pitchers. He told Durocher once, *"Give me some strong, young arms, and I'll give you a winning pitching staff."* Working with a staff of mostly rookies and sophomores the previous year, Joe proved his point. Before joining the Cubs, Joe was the pitching coach for the Cardinals and Dodgers. He was given a good deal of credit for the development of Sandy Koufax. Before that time, Joe managed 9 seasons in the International and Western Leagues. He was a catcher in his playing days and caught at Cleveland and the New York Giants when military service in World War II ended his playing career.

Durocher had already lifted Joe Niekro for a pinch hitter the prior inning, and Becker told me I would be pitching the seventh inning. He gave me pat on the back and told me to get the job done. As I walked out to the mound, the announcer said, *"Now pitching for Chicago, number 38: Darcy Fast."* My name reverberated around the stadium. I walked out to the mound and I heard the fans booing, which was an honor. They weren't booing that vigorously, but when 25,000 people boo it can sound pretty loud.

I felt a little off balance and overwhelmed, and tried to look around to get my bearings. I glanced out to center field and noticed the Braves had a totem pole out there. The team's mascot, an Indian Brave, was dancing around the pole. I don't know if he was supposed to be putting a hex on me or what. The lights were glaring, but I felt pretty good. The scripture verse my Dad shared with me years ago came to my mind—"I can do everything through Him who gives me strength." I realized I was about to pitch in the major leagues.

Our catcher, Randy Hundley, came out and we went over the signs real quickly. I told him the pitches I threw, I took my allocated warm up pitches, and that was it. Hundley, I knew, was one of the best catchers the Cubs ever had. He'd come to the team in a trade in 1966 that also brought Bill Hands. Hundley was a good hitter, but was known to be one of the best fielding catchers in the late 60's. He'd won the Gold Glove in 1967, committing just four errors. He was also known for having amazing endurance, and since Durocher rarely rested his players, he worked Hundley as hard as anyone. Randy set a record in 1968 with 160 games behind the plate, completing 147 of them! That's an amazing record, considering how much wear and tear catchers endure. He was also the first player to catch 150 games for three consecutive years (1967-1969). Hundley was also one of the few catchers to ever steal home, something he did in 1966 against Gary Kroll of the Houston Astros. He also hit for the cycle on August 11 of that year.

I was pretty nervous, there's no question about it, and I'm not sure how many of my warm-up pitches hit the strike zone, but seeing Hundley behind the plate helped a little. He came back out, went over the signs before the first batter, and he said to me, *"Darcy, just relax. Just think about where you were pitching last year."* Little did he know that a year before I had pitched in only one professional game in the Pioneer League, and up to that point had pitched in only 25 minor league games.

I only pitched against two batters that night, but they were great hitters — Aaron and Johnson. One popped up for my first out, and I walked the other. Everything happened so fast. Durocher immediately came out of the dugout and walked toward the mound to take me out of the game. I'd never made such a quick entrance and exit in my entire career, but I figured that's the way Durocher was going to use me — just in short, key situations, mostly against lefties. Phil Reagan came in after me and the game went into extra innings, tied 2-2. In the 10th, the Braves scored on a base hit over the head of our first baseman Ernie Banks and the speedy Felix Millan flew around the bases and scored. It was Phil Regan's first loss of the season.

I was actually grateful to Durocher for getting me right into a game. That really helped me get rid of the jitters, and even though I didn't last very long, it made me feel like I could pitch in the majors.

After the game and on our way back to the hotel, Jack Griffin from the Sun Times sat next to me and started asking me a bunch of questions. He had a little pad and was writing everything down, so I knew he was writing an article for the paper. Here's what came out in the Sun Times a few days later:

"He always thought he was a better basketball player, the tall kid with the peaches and cream complexion said, than he was a baseball thrower. . . But there he was, Darcy Rae Fast, 21, 6 feet 3, 195 pounds, sitting in the Cubs' dressing room, wearing a major league uniform. A little shy, perhaps, still not sure all of this had really happened. . . Less than a week ago, Fast was throwing for a little piece of obscurity named Lodi in the California League, riding the night buses, staying in the walk-up hotels, grabbing hamburgers. . . Last week, he hung his clothes on a hook in a locker room the size of a phone booth, or came to the yard already dressed in the bus. And now it was steak, and jet planes, and a dressing stall all his own. . . but for now he is working with the big guys, an impossible dream no matter how short the dance, and that's not bad for a kid who doesn't even have a year of professional baseball hanging from his belt. . . They let him have a look at the way major league baseball is played, even let him throw a little in combat. Saturday he got one man out, and lost the other on a walk, and then took the long walk."

And that's the way it would go the rest of the season. They would call me in against left-handed hitters, let me pitch to a batter or two, and that was it. I had prepared my entire life to play in the majors, reached a point where I thought it would never happen, and then my dream sprang back to life. Suddenly, I was really doing it. I was playing in the major leagues, and I couldn't have been happier.

A.J. & Ethel Fast and their two boys – Dallas & Darcy.
This picture was taken when dad was pastor of the Irving Park
Church of God in Portland, Oregon.

The start of my basketball and baseball days at Lacey Grade School. I played center on the 7th grade basketball team and first base on the baseball team. We were the Lacey Lions.

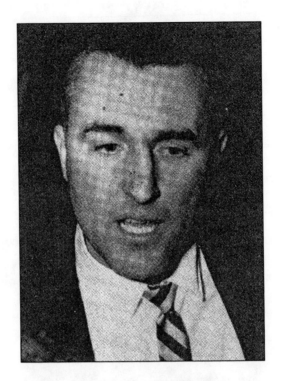

Archie McCallum—
My high school teacher and basketball coach.
He encouraged me to work hard at developing
my natural athletic ability. I will always be grateful
for his influence and leadership in my life.

Shooting a jump-shot and taking the ball to the hoop
for the North Thurston High School Rams. Basketball was
my favorite sport in high school.

Standing between some of my teammates at North
Thurston High School and (below) our cheerleading staff—JoAnn
is kneeling in the front row—second from left.

Jim Fouts—One of the most respected and successful high school coaches in Washington state history. I took great pride in playing football and baseball for him.

Mom and Dad with me after a high school football game.
We were smiling so we must have won!

Dr. E. Joe Gilliam — pastor, college president, church leader, and lifetime friend. He made a lasting impression on my life and encouraged me to pursue a professional baseball career and later to commit my life to the ministry.

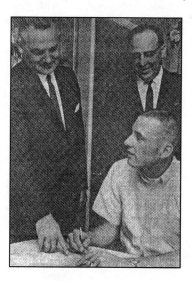

Signing my first professional baseball contract with the Chicago Cubs — scout George Freese and dad looking on. What a great day!

Getting ready to deliver a pitch for the Warner Pacific Knights baseball team and standing with Coach Gary Aved and our college basketball team. We were a small Christian college, but surprised a lot of teams with our ability to compete.

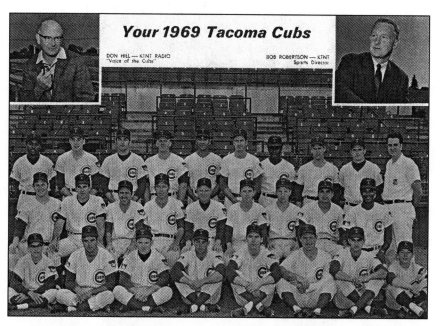

Standing in the back row (second from left) with the Tacoma
Cubs—1969 Pacific Coast League Champions and radio
announcers—Don Hill & Bob Robertson from KTNT Radio.

JoAnn and I were married in the Olympia-Lacey Church of God on June 1, 1968. It was a rainy day, but that made little difference to us. We were just happy to be together.

My dad officiated at our wedding and many of our family and friends participated.

On our way to face the world together! We drove to Lodi, CA the
next day for me to rejoin the team and start our married
lives together, but two weeks later I was pitching with the
Chicago Cubs. JoAnn drove back to Olympia and would
later meet me in Chicago.

My official Chicago Cubs picture taken shortly
after joining the team in June, 1968.

Pitching in my first game with the Cubs
against the Atlanta Braves.

Fred Martin and myself shortly before a game. He taught me how
to pitch and had a great influence on my career. We remained good
friends even when I was traded to the San Diego Padres.

Kneeling down to have my picture taken in the outfield at
Wrigley Field—an amazing place to start my major league career.
Cub fans are the greatest baseball fans in the world!

Shortly before my first appearance as a relief pitcher for the Cubs at Wrigley Field—that day I faced the St. Louis Cardinals.

My rookie baseball card came out in 1972. The picture was taken when I played with the Chicago Cubs and the cap was changed to look like the San Diego Padres.

My oldest son and his family—Chris, Dyan, McKailey & Madison, and my youngest son and his family –Bryce, Kami, Alyx and Taber. They are a great blessing to our lives!

The Fast family at our church in Centralia.
We enjoy many great times together!

Chapter 6

The Majors

I next game I pitched in was on Sunday, June 23rd, 1968 against
the Cincinnati Reds. Bill Hands was the starter. It was a rainy
day, a doubleheader, and it was in old Crosley Field in Cincinnati.
The original name of the park, built in 1911, was Redland Field.
It was one of those wonderful old parks built during the early part
of the twentieth century. Incidentally, the Cubs' Wrigley Field and
Boston's Fenway Park were also built around the same time. Crosley
was one of the smallest parks in the league and could only accom-
modate about 30,000 fans. It also had an unusual outfield—the grass
sloped up to the fence as a kind of warning barrier for the outfielders.
Incidentally, the park in Houston now has a sloping hill like that.
Crosley stayed in use until June 26, 1970.

The game got off to a late start because it rained all afternoon,
leaving large puddles all over the outfield. The sky was gray and
cloudy, as we fell behind three runs in the first inning. Bill Hands

walked Pete Rose on four pitches, which was unusual because Hands had great control. Alex Johnson then hit a single and Vada Pinson followed with a bouncer toward first base. It looked like Ernie Banks would be able to make a play on it, but the ball took a big bounce and went off of Banks' glove and into the outfield. Tony Perez followed up with a hard single to left. Pinson scored when Johnny Bench—a rookie that year—hit into a double play. Unfortunately, we weren't really able to get anything going the whole game, though Billy Williams clubbed a home run in the fourth, a line drive over the fence in right center. By the time I entered the game in the eighth, we were trailing 7-1. It was eight days since I last pitched, and not pitching regularly was one of the biggest adjustments I had to make in the major leagues. I was used to pitching seven to nine innings every four days. As I entered the game, I was more concerned about my control because I hadn't pitched in over a week. Tony Perez was the first batter I faced, and he dug into the batter's box. He was an intimidating hitter, and of course went on to a Hall of Fame career. It was his fourth year in the big leagues, and he already had a good reputation. I threw him a hard, sinking fastball and he grounded out to Kessinger, our shortstop. Next up was Johnny Bench, another future Hall of Famer. He lined out hard to left on another fastball. Their first baseman, Lee May, who was *not* a future Cooperstown inductee despite a very good seventeen year major league career, was up next. I threw a couple of curve balls and he flew out to center. I walked off the mound feeling confident. I had pitched a perfect inning in the big leagues and felt I might have a long major league career.

I met Pete Rose after the game and spoke to him briefly. We were both coming out the clubhouse and walking toward the player's parking lot, where our bus was waiting and his car was parked. He asked me how long I'd been with the Cubs. As soon as I'd answered, he jumped into his yellow corvette and peeled out of the parking lot. Pete was a guy that many of the other ball players didn't care for. Maybe they were jealous of him. Many didn't like the way he ran out every base on balls as if he'd hit a single. They called him Charlie Hustle for a reason. In our game that day, he ran out a walk and some of the guys on the bench gave him a bad time, razzing him pretty good. They didn't have a lot of love for Pete Rose (nobody really did), but he was still a great ball player.

Vada Pinson played center for the Reds that day, and that had a special meaning to me. Pinson played in the majors for eighteen years, from 1958 through 1975. His best years were with the Reds, from '58 to '68. He had an incredible combination of power, speed, and defense, and he led the National League twice in hits (1961, 1963), in doubles (1959, 1960), and twice in triples (1963, 1967). He batted .343 in 1961, when the Reds won the NL pennant. He was a great center fielder who threw and hit left handed. After leaving the Reds, he played for the St. Louis Cardinals, Cleveland Indians, California Angels, and Kansas City Royals, and ended his career with 2,757 hits and a career batting average of .286, with 256 home runs and 305 stolen bases. Later, he became a coach for the

Seattle Mariners, Detroit Tigers and Florida Marlins. Unfortunately, he died of a stroke in 1995. He went to the same high school in Oakland, McClymonds High School, that Hall of Fame outfielder Frank Robinson and Basketball Hall of Fame center Bill Russell attended.

Years earlier, when I was 9 years old, I won a paper route contest and got to travel up to Seattle to old Sick's Stadium to see the Rainiers of the Pacific Coast league. Vada Pinson caught my eye immediately, because he was just a great ballplayer and it was obvious just from the way he moved. I idolized him. While I was in the stands, Pinson hit a foul ball that hit me in the leg. Little did I know that I'd be playing against him in the second game I'd pitch in the major leagues. I never had the opportunity to talk to him, though I wish I would have.

By now JoAnn and I had found a furnished apartment in Schiller Park near O'Hara Airport in Chicago. Several other players and their wives were also living there, including Bill and Sandy Hands, and Bill and Robin Plumber. JoAnn became friends with the other wives and they gave her a birthday party on her 21st. One day, she went to the game with some of the players wives, and they were standing by the pass gate to get tickets at Wrigley field. She went up to the attendant and said, "I'd like tickets for Plumber's Fast Hands. The attendant started laughing, along with everyone else who heard it.

JoAnn has always loved animals, and I gave her a chocolate poodle—Coco Bean—to keep her company while we were on the road playing games. One time when she went to O'Hara to pick me up after a road trip, she left Coco in our apartment and he started barking so much that someone got into our apartment and let him out. When we came back that evening, we couldn't find him. I spent the next three days before and after our games looking for him. I finally located him after a young man had found him and gave him to his parents in downtown Chicago. We were doubtful that we would ever see him again. From that point on, she carried Coco in her purse to Wrigley Field for our games.

The Curse of the Billy Goat

We discovered later that JoAnn wasn't the only one that had brought a pet to Wrigley Field, though. On October 6, 1945, William "Billy Goat" Sianis, a Greek immigrant, had two $7.20 box seat tickets to watch Game 4 of the 1945 World Series between the Chicago Cubs and the Detroit Tigers. Sianis brought along Murphy, his pet goat, and entered Wrigley Field.

Sianis took the goat on the playing field before the start of the game, but was eventually lead off the field by the ushers. After a lot of complaining, Sainis and his goat were allowed to use their box seats for the game. However, due to the animal's intolerable odor, Cubs owner Philip K. Wrigley ordered that they be driven out of the stadium before the game was over. William Sianis was upset after being forced to leave the stadium, and allegedly placed a curse on the Cubs so that they'd never win another pennant and would not play in another World Series at Wrigley Field. The Cubs finally lost the 1945 World Series, and have not made it back to the championship series since. Sianis died in 1970, leaving his curse on the Cubs. Since that time, and with so many losing seasons, the Curse of the Billy Goat slowly became an urban legend. For the next twenty seasons, the Cubs finished in the league's second division until the streak was finally ended in 1967 when Duroucher became the club's manager. In 1969, the Cubs lost an eight and a half game lead in the National League's Eastern Division, but finished second to the New York Mets, who won both the National League Championship Series and the World Series. In the 1973 season, the Cubs lost 49 of their last 76 games. The Cubs were again in a good position to win the division for the first time in 1984, but they finally lost to the San Diego Padres 3 games to 2. In the 1989 season, the Cubs won the NL East but lost in the Championship Series 4 games to 1 to the San Francisco Giants.

The curse seemed to leave the Cubs when they led the World Series champion Florida Marlins 3 games to 2 in the National League Championship Series at Wrigley Field. They had a 3-0 lead in Game 6 with only five outs to place them in the World Series, but still under the spell of the curse, lost the last game to the Marlins 9 to 6. The Marlins won the National League Championship and advanced to play in the World Series against the New York Yankees. The curse continued to show up again in the 2004 season. The Cubs were playing with a 1 and half game lead in the National League wild card. They played against the New York Mets and won the first game, but lost the next two games. They went on to lose to the Braves and were eliminated from playoff contention.

Mr. Wrigley, the Cubs' owner, had decided to add lights to Wrigley Field in 1942, but after the Japanese attack on Pearl Harbor, he instead donated the materials intended for lighting Wrigley Field to the war effort. He eventually decided never to install lights for a variety of reasons, so Wrigley remained the only ball park in the major leagues to only play day games until the Chicago Tribune purchased the Cubs in 1981. The city of Chicago had passed an ordinance banning night events at Wrigley Field, due to its presence in a residential neighborhood, so the Tribune Company was unable to install lights until the ordinance was repealed. The first major league night game at Wrigley was played on August 9, 1988 against the New York Mets, ending a streak of 5,687 consecutive home day games. Actually, the first night game was scheduled the day before, but was postponed because of rain. On that day, several Cubs players were having fun sliding on the rain soaked tarp and were fined $500 each by Don Zimmer, the Cubs' manager and my former manager at Salt Lake City.

My Greatest Major League Experience

In those days, there wasn't a fifteen day disabled list, so if you got hurt, you just kept playing. A lot of times, guys played with a lot of pain. Glenn Beckert, our second baseman, had the longest hitting streak in baseball that year, and he fought through a lot of little nicks and cuts. Becker, a four-time All-Star, was actually having his best year in 1968: he ended up leading the league in runs and went on to win the Gold Glove Award. The sports writers, particularly *Sports Illustrated,* were really following him carefully, and there was a lot of pressure on him during the streak: when his batting streak started getting into the thirties, everybody started talking about Joe DiMaggio's 56 game consecutive hitting streak—a record that most people in baseball believe will never be broken. I remember one time, Durocher got mad at some of the sports writers before a game. He leveled them all because they wanted a statement from Beckert, and he told them to get out of the dugout and to not come back until they were invited back.

The team went on a seven game losing streak at the end of June, and everyone's mood soured. We really needed a win, though it didn't seem likely that it would come against the St Louis Cardinals. They were the defending National League and World Champions, and had some of the best players in the league: Lou Brock, Curt Flood, Orlando Cepeda, and Tim McCarver, for example.

Ron Santo was struggling more than other guys during the losing streak, and it was eating him up. He was the team captain and a real fiery guy—no one questioned his leadership. One time, he asked me if I had ever played against any high school teams from Seattle. He graduated from Roosevelt High School in Seattle, and since I was from Olympia (Lacey), he thought maybe I had played against some of the schools he played against. The fact that we were both from

Washington made me feel like we had a special connection with each other.

Santo was in a slump, and was almost driven to tears because of his own lack of performance in the previous day's game. Santo was a great player who was named to nine All-Star teams during his fifteen year career. He also won five straight Gold Glove awards (1964-1968). He'd come into the league with the Cubs in 1960, and went on to play for the team through '73. He finished his career with the crosstown White Sox, which must have broken a few hearts. He had very good power, and during his fourteen years with the Cubs, he hit 337 home runs. He was also the first third baseman to hit over 300 home runs and win five Gold Gloves. Mike Schmidt, of course, went on to surpass those numbers. Santo also got some notoriety for his choice of batting helmets. In 1966, during a hitting streak, he was beaned and sidelined for two weeks. When he returned, he wore a batting helmet with an ear flap, and those helmets have since become standard for all ballplayers.

Santo had Type 1 diabetes, but he was afraid if people found out, he'd be forced to retire. Consequently, he hid the disease. However, he revealed that he had always struggled with the disease on August 28th, 1971 as part of "Ron Santo Day" at Wrigley Field. He'd had diabetes since he was 18 and had been told he would only live 25 years. Since retirement, he's had both legs amputated below the knee, but is still going strong as a Cubs broadcaster on WGN. The Cubs retired Santo's number in 2003. He was only the third Cub's player to receive that honor – the other two were Ernie Banks and

Billy Williams. Santo has come within a hair of making it to the Hall of Fame, and many, including myself, feel he deserves to get in. He came within five votes in 2007.

The game with the Cardinals got off to a good start and it looked like we would easily snap our losing streak. We scored two in the first after a walk, followed by singles by Glenn Beckert and Santo and a ground out. In the second, Hundley started things with a single, and center fielder Adolfo Philips followed with a single, but was out trying to stretch it into a double. Durocher was furious, because Philips didn't run full bore to first and didn't even slide into second. He came into the clubhouse and the first thing out of his mouth was, "In the first place he (Philips) didn't run hard going to first base, then he didn't run hard going to second, and finally he didn't slide. We can't play baseball that way and win, and if anyone else plays like that, I'll fine him too!" Durocher ended up fining Philips $200. It was only the second time in Durocher's career that he'd ever fined a player.

The wheels fell off in the second, and we all thought our misery was going to continue. Joe Niekro, our starter, got hammered in the third. St. Louis pounded out five straight hits, including a double by the inimitable Lou Brock, after the first batter had struck out. Durocher took Niekro out and replaced him with Jack Lamabe, but he didn't fare any better, though he managed to get the second out of the inning. Bill Stoneman came in and finally settled things down, but not before the Cardinals had taken a 6-3 lead. We were pretty shell shocked.

In the sixth inning, we were down 6-4 and still clinging to life. Stoneman was pitching well, but got into a big jam in the sixth. After a groundout, he gave up a walk, and then hurt his own cause by throwing away a ball hit back to him. Brock singled to left to push across another Cardinals run, though we got the second out of the inning on a perfect relay to third. Stoneman walked Curt Flood, however, putting runners on first and second with two outs. Durocher had seen enough. I was warming up in the bullpen and with lefty Tim McCarver due up, he called on me.

McCarver was having a great season and was hitting around .340 at the time. I knew when I came into the game I needed to get the guy out. I was getting used to checking the line-up for left-handed hitters because those were the guys I most likely would face in the game. I knew how well McCarver was hitting and how important it was to get out of the inning without giving up any more runs, if we had a chance to win. As I walked to the pitcher's mound, I felt a sense of pride and excitement. This was my first appearance at Wrigley Field in front of 30,000 Cub fans. The announcer said, *"Now pitching for Chicago, #38: Darcy Fast,"* and I received a nice ovation from the crowd. Here I was, pitching in Wrigley on the same mound that Dizzy Dean had pitched to Babe Ruth when he pointed to right field and hit the most memorable homerun of his career. I couldn't believe it. Now I was facing the World Champion St. Louis Cardinals!

It felt good that Durocher had confidence in me to get it done as he gave me the ball, and told me how to pitch to him. He said to keep the ball away and to throw him curve balls. The first pitch I threw was a curve ball, and I was surprised at how bad McCarver looked swinging at the pitch. I remember Phil Regan told me once that good hitters will purposely looked fooled by a pitch sometimes so that the pitcher will throw the same pitch. When the batter is looking for the same pitch, he has a better chance of hitting it. I wondered if McCarver was doing that to me. When Hundley called for another curve, I motioned for him to come out to the mound to discuss it with me. I didn't want to show him up by calling for a different pitch. He told me that I needed to throw him another curve with something on it. I did, and he swung through it for strike two. Now, I was sure Hundley wanted me to waste a pitch outside, but instead he called for the curve again. I think McCarver was surprised at the seeing the same pitch again because he hit a little grounder to Ernie Banks at first base, and when I covered first, Ernie tossed it to me. That retired the side. It could have been a big inning for the Cardinals and I felt good that I'd done my job. I didn't think much about it, since it was a pretty short appearance. Only in the bottom half of the inning, our bats finally exploded. Hundley popped out to the catcher to start the inning, but after Philips walked, Durocher sent Al Spangler in to pinch hit for me. Philips advanced on a wild pitch and then scored when Spangler singled to right. Don Kessinger popped out, but then Glenn Beckert singled to right. Billy Williams singled to left, pushing across another run, and our bench started to come alive. Santo stepped to the plate. He hadn't hit a home run in fourteen games and he was overdue. He smashed a three-run dinger over the wall, and everyone leaped out of the dugout to celebrate and congratulate him. We pushed across another run, and suddenly we were leading 10-7. And it dawned on me: I was the pitcher of record. If we could hold on, I'd get my first major league win.

Phil Regan came in and pitched the final three innings, giving up only one unearned run. The monkey was off our back—we won 10-8 and I had played an important part. Jack Brickhouse, the Cubs TV announcer, asked me if I could give him a short interview after the game. He started out by saying, "With me today is rookie pitcher Darcy Fast, who just won his first major league game against the St. Louis Cardinals." After the interview, he gave me a gift certificate for a pair of shoes at a men's store in Chicago. When I came into the club house, the players came by my locker and were congratulating me. Regan said I did a great job under a lot of pressure, and congratulated me on my first major league win. Santo patted me on the butt and said, "Nice job rookie," A number of sports writers came over to my locker and asked me a few more questions. I was, of course, ecstatic. That game made me feel part of the team. But the official scorer for the game had other ideas, and he did something that is almost never done—he gave the win to Phil Regan. Here's what they said in the Chicago Tribune the next day:

"Darcy Rae Fast, rookie lefthander, was sent in to halt a Cardinal rally in the sixth after a walk, Stoneman's throwing

error and a single by Brock netted an unearned run. Fast used three pitches to handle Tim McCarver on a grounder, thus retiring the side. But the brevity of his assignment—however perfect—was deemed to have been dwarfed by Regan's three innings that followed. Thus Darcy did not get credit for the triumph despite qualifying technically."

That was a huge disappointment. Even Phil Regan was sympathetic, and offered me encouragement. He was one of the pitchers on the team I felt I could go to with questions about opposing batters, so I appreciated his pat on the back. He was a very smart and crafty guy.

Phil's nickname, "the Vulture," was given to him by the great Sandy Koufax because he picked up so many wins by pitching in short relief. He played for the Detroit Tigers, Los Angeles Dodgers, Cubs, and briefly for the Chicago White Sox in his thirteen year career. He made 105 starts over that time and pitched in 551 games. His best season came with the Dodgers in 1966, when he went 14-1 with a 1.62 ERA and 88 strikeouts in 116 innings pitched as a reliever. You can see what Koufax meant! He went 96-81 with a 3.84 ERA and 92 saves in his career, and he had 743 strikeouts in 1372 innings pitched.

The Vulture was famous for loading up the baseball with all kinds of gunk that would make it nearly impossible to hit. It had never occurred to me to try something like that because I'd never met anyone who'd done it, but everyone knew Phil threw a very good spitball. And he usually got away with it. I first learned what "slippery elm" was from him. It's a little tablet you put on your tongue that turns your saliva into a kind of mucus. That's how Phil would load up his pitches.

Besides slippery elm, Phil also used Vaseline. He'd hide the Vaseline on different parts of his uniform: he'd have some on the bill of his hat, in the fold of his glove or in his shoes. He would reach down to tie his shoes and grab a little Vaseline. He'd keep it underneath his pants. He had seven or eight different places where he would keep the stuff. And every time he went out there, when he needed a big pitch, everyone knew he was going to load up one of those balls. I'll tell you what—the other players knew it, too, because they were always complaining. The umpires were always stopping the game and going out to try and find where Phil was hiding the illegal substances. It was clear to them that the ball was moving in unnatural ways, but they had a hard time finding out how he was doing it.

A couple of times, the umpires actually took some strikes away from him. They'd say, "If it happens again, you're out of the ball-game." Durocher would run out to the field and start chewing out the umpires. He would stand between Phil Regan and the umpire and argue for as long as possible, and in the meantime, Phil would be hiding the Vaseline. I never tried it because I was just trying to get comfortable in the major leagues. Every time I went to a ballpark, it was a new park. Every time I pitched against a batter, it was a new batter. Every situation was new. That's one of the biggest adjustments you have to make when you go to the majors—instead of pitching in front of five or six thousand people, you're pitching in front of thousands and thousands. So I wasn't about to try throwing a spitter.

Jimmy Durante and George Jessel

On Sunday, June 30th, 1968, Jimmy Durante and George Jessel, two old time actors, visited Durocher at Wrigley Field. They presented him with a large, 24-karat gold-plated four leaf clover, for luck. We could have used some of that luck on Tuesday, our next game, when we lost to the Phillies, a game in which I made my third major league appearance. It was "Canada Day" and the Winnepeg city police pipe band played as part of the opening ceremonies, celebrating Canada's Independence Day. Ferguson Jenkins, a Canadian, was honored as the Canadian player of the year.

Jenkins was one of the few guys that I had a hard time connecting with in the majors. It was nothing personal, but he was just hard to get to know. One time, I walked into the locker room and he was shaving his face with a butter knife. I guess he wanted to look good, but I had no idea why he wasn't using a razor.

I asked him what he was doing and he said, "I'm shaving, man. I'm shaving," and told me to get lost.

I shrugged and walked away. He seemed aloof and never wanted to get involved in any long conversations, especially with a rookie. But he was a great pitcher. Born in Ontario, Canada, in 1943, he pitched for the Cubs for the majority of his nineteen year career, though he bounced around a little and also played for the Philadelphia Phillies, Texas Rangers, and Boston Red Sox. He was originally drafted by the Phillies in 1963 and made his debut in the majors as a 21-year old in 1965 as a reliever—the same age I was in '68. He was traded the next year to the Cubs, along with Adolpho Phillips and John Hartenstein, for pitchers Larry Jackson and Bob Buhl. It's one of the greatest trades in Cubs history, because Jenkins turned into one of the best pitchers in the majors. In his first full year starting in 1967, he won twenty games, struck out 236 and managed a 2.80 ERA. He finished tied for second in the Cy Young voting. Mike McCormick of the San Francisco Giants won it that year.

In 1968, Jenkins was having an even better year, which may be why he seemed a little aloof to me. He won twenty again that year and his ERA dropped to 2.63, and he struck out an impressive 260 batters.

Jenkins and Durocher used to really get into it, arguing back and forth. One time Jenkins was pitching, and Durocher walked out to the mound and they got into big argument. No one could figure out why they were fighting—the only probable reason was that Durocher didn't like his attitude on the mound. Durocher felt as though he always had to ride Jenkins to get him to play at his best.

Jenkins best season was in 1971. He won the NL Cy Young, and even finished seventh in the MVP voting. He went 24-13 with a 2.77 ERA and 263 strikeouts. He was the first Cub pitcher and the first

Canadian ever to win the Cy Young. He could also hit, and rang up a .478 slugging percentage in 1971, with an amazing six home runs. He drove in twenty runs in just 115 at-bats. On September 1st of 1971, Jenkins threw a complete game against the Montreal Expos, hit two home runs, and almost single handedly won the game, 5-2. He finished the season completing 30 of 39 starts, while walking only 37 the entire year in 325 innings pitched. Jenkins led the league in wins twice, fewest walks per 9 innings five times, complete games nine times, and home runs allowed seven times. He won twenty or more games for six straight seasons (1967-1972) which was the longest streak since Warren Spahn had done it from 1956 to 1961.

Jenkins also got into a bit of trouble later in his career. In 1980, during a customs inspection in Toronto, he was found in possession of cocaine and marijuana. The commissioner, Bowie Kuhn, suspended him and he missed the rest of that season. An independent arbiter reinstated him, however, and he returned the next year and continued playing until his retirement following the 1983 season. After he retired from the Majors, he pitched for two seasons for the London Majors of the Intercounty Major Baseball League in Ontario. Fergie was inducted into the Canadian Baseball Hall of Fame in 1987 and into the Major League Hall in 1991. He was the first Canadian ever to be elected to Cooperstown. One interesting bit of trivia: the Phillies traded both Jenkins and Ryne Sandberg (in 1982) to the Cubs. The Phillies, in essence, gave the Cubs two of their greatest players, and two Hall of Famers.

On June 30th, the team honored Jenkins, and everything past that ceremony was all downhill. Edgar Munzel of the Chicago Sun-Times wrote, *"The kilted band probably wouldn't have done any worse than the Cubs defensively, even if they had used their bagpipes as gloves."*

Rich Nye was our starter that day, and a guy I really got along with. He and I shared an apartment before JoAnn arrived in Chicago, and he was the guy I felt most comfortable going to with questions about how to pitch to certain players. He helped me an awful lot with the mental approach to the game. In the minor leagues you could get away with throwing the wrong pitch a lot of the time because the hitters weren't as good as they were in the majors. Rich deserved a better fate that day — he was lifted in the sixth for a pinch hitter, though he hadn't given up an earned run. In the first, with two out and a base runner on first, Richie Allen singled to center. The ball skipped past Adolfo Philips in center field, allowing one run to score. In the second, Ron Santo fumbled a grounder with two outs, and another run came across on a wild pitch. Two innings, two unearned runs. We weren't finished. In the sixth, Ernie Banks misplayed a grounder that allowed another run to cross the plate. We rallied for two in the bottom of the inning, but never managed to recover, though we again rallied in the ninth for two runs. However, the game was still within reach at 5-2 when I entered with runners on first and third and two outs in the seventh inning. Durocher brought me in to face their left handed first baseman, Johnny Briggs. I didn't know much about him, so I stuck to my best pitches. I struck him out and felt pretty good about myself. Now I had two good back-to-back appearances and I was gaining more confidence to pitch in the major leagues.

At that point in the season, the Cubs were in ninth place, 13 games out of first, with a 33-42 record. We had won only 3 games since I joined the team, and only Houston trailed us in the standings. Losing affects everyone, of course, and a lot of the guys were pretty cranky and upset. More was expected of that team, but we just couldn't figure out how to get a winning streak going. Ernie Banks, who was 37 and toward the tail end of his career, was the only guy who never got dispirited. That guy always had a smile on his face, and it was something I found amazing and truly inspiring.

Ernie "Mr. Cub" Banks played his entire career with the Chicago Cubs. From 1953 to 1971, he made it to eleven All-Star games, and was elected to the Baseball Hall of Fame in 1977. Ernie originally signed with the Kansas City Monarchs of the Negro League in 1950 and broke into the majors in 1953. He was the Cubs' first black player. He started off as a shortstop and moved to first base in 1962, as his range at short began to diminish. He's one of only four Cubs to have his number (14) retired by the team. The others are Ron Santo (10), Billy Williams (26) and Ryne Sandberg (23).

Banks was just a fabulous guy. Most of the veterans kept their distance from rookies—for all they knew, we could be sent back to the minors any day—but the first time I entered the club house, Ernie Banks came right up and introduced himself. He took me around and introduced me to all of the other ball players, and to some of the writers for <u>The Tribune</u> and <u>The Sun Times</u>. He tried to make me feel as comfortable as possible, and he did that with every player, particularly the young guys who'd just joined the team.

He is still known for his famous catch phrase, *"It's a beautiful day for a ballgame... Let's play two!"* When he said it, though, he meant it, because he would have played baseball all day if someone let him. In 1955, he set the record for grand slams in a season with 5. That record stood until Don Mattingly of the Yankees hit 6 in 1987. He also won the National League Most Valuable Player Award twice, in 1958 and 1959, even though the Cubs weren't in the running either of those years. Banks finished his career with 512 home runs, the most ever by a shortstop, and still holds the record for the most extra base hits by a Cub—1,009.

Banks was also the first black manager in baseball, though only on a technicality. When he retired, the Cubs took him on as a coach. On May 8th, 1973, Cubs manager Whitey Lockman, my old Tacoma skipper, was thrown out of the game. Banks filled in as manager for the remaining two innings of a 12-inning 3-2 win over the San Diego Padres.

During the late 1960s and early 1970s, Ernie owned a car dealership called "Ernie Banks Ford" on Stoney Island Avenue in Chicago, so he always drove a nice new car himself. One day, after the game, he asked me if I had any transportation. I told him I didn't, and he said, "Well, you can use my car." He gave me the keys to his LTD—it was brand new and sitting out in the players' parking lot. I was stunned. After dressing, I walked out to the lot with JoAnn.

There must have been 100 or 200 people in the players' parking lot waiting for Banks to sign autographs. When they saw me open up Ernie's car they started shouting.

"You're not Ernie Banks! What are you doing taking his car?" They were pretty mad, too.

Later, I figured out that Ernie did that with all the young ball players. That way he wouldn't have to stand there and sign autographs. Not that he wouldn't. He was just a great guy and he'd stand there for hours if he had to, but loaning out his car gave him a chance to get a breather once in a while. He'd take off through another entrance of the ballpark, catch a cab and head home, free as a bird. He let me use his car as long as I needed it.

He was also the guy that would try to pick me up if I was getting discouraged. Some of the players couldn't remember who I was, but Ernie knew exactly. One time, after I'd had a rough game, Ernie came up to me and said, *"Keep working hard—you'll make it around here."* When you're playing in the majors, most guys are not concerned about you. They're concerned about how they're doing and how the team is going. Ernie was the kind of guy that'd put his arm around you and say, *"You did a good job out there tonight."* It felt great to have somebody like that in your corner.

Yosh

When you're in the clubhouse before or after a game, if you have a little bit of time, you're supposed to autograph baseballs. The Cubs would get everyone to sign them, then sell them or use them for promotion. The clubhouse manager, Yosh Kawano, had been there for years. He put a bunch of balls next to me one day and said, "Sign these," and so I began to sign away. After I signed about two or three dozen of them, Yosh came over, took one look at where I'd been signing and nearly flew off the handle.

He said, *"You can't sign right there!"*

I didn't see how it mattered.

"Why did you sign the balls right there?" He looked like someone had just stolen his pet dog.

I said, *"What do you mean 'right there'?* I just signed the ball just like everybody else."

"The sweet part, the narrow part of the seams, is always reserved for the manager," he said.

I was signing where Leo Durocher was supposed to sign his name, but nobody had bothered to tell me that. (They kept the balls, but no one mentioned it to Durocher. They knew better.)

Chewed out

Leo Durocher was not a warm and cuddly player's manager. He was a gritty, nail-spitting type who almost never talked to the younger players and spent a lot time in the clubhouse playing cards with Ron Santo and Glenn Beckert, his buddies. Most of the rookies felt intimidated by him, and I think he liked that. He knew he had power over us, and he acted as if he didn't care what people thought. He was a big name in the sport at the time, and he had a big chip on his shoulder, like he was always trying to prove something. He liked to argue. He would chew umpires out. He would chew his own players out.

He got after me in one game. It was July 4th, the second game of a doubleheader against the Phillies, and there was a huge crowd at Wrigley. We'd won the first game, 6-2, and felt pretty good about ourselves. One of my high school coaches, Mike Donahue, was there with his wife. He'd left high school teaching and was working at Purdue University at the time. Billy Williams had an amazing day. He slammed a home run in the first game, and drove in all four of our runs in the second game with a three-run homer and a single. In fact, we managed only three hits off of rookie Jeff James and reliever Johnny Boozer, with Glenn Beckert getting the third hit with a double. The home runs for Williams, 7 and 8 for the season, gave him 206 for his career and moved him past Bill Nicholson into fourth place on the all-time Cubs homer list.

For a while in that game, it looked like James, a career minor leaguer, might toss a no-hitter against us. He didn't give up his first hit until there was one out in the sixth. Of course, after a hit batsman and a walk, Williams crushed a homer and actually tied the score at three. Our starter, Bill Hands, pitched the first three innings and got knocked around a little, giving up three runs. Durocher, feeling the game slipping away, brought me in. I held the fort for three solid innings, striking out four, and I felt untouchable. But the wheels fell off in the seventh. I gave up a single and double to start the inning. After a walk and a sacrifice fly, I gave up a double to Johnny Briggs, the left handed first baseman for the Phillies. Durocher came storming out of the dugout and started screaming

"How can you give up a hit to a lefty, Fast? How the (blank) can you do that?" His face was red and you could just about see the steam pouring out of his ears. He was disgusted and he didn't just ask for the ball, he ripped it out of my hand. Until that point, I'd had a chance to earn my first major league win, but instead I got my first loss. The article in the Chicago Sun-Times made it seem as if Durocher was pleased with my outing, but I definitely didn't get that feeling:

"Darcy Fast, young southpaw rookie, pitched brilliantly for three innings and then was rapped for four runs in the seventh to lose his first big league decision. His pitching and also that of Gary Ross, another youngster who pitched the last two innings, was highly gratifying to Durocher."

I felt like I'd let the team down a little bit, but I'd also shown that I belonged in the big leagues. Ernie Banks patted me on the back and told me I did a good job, and that made me feel good. Billy Williams also offered me some solace.

Billy Williams

I really liked Billy Williams. That doubleheader in July was not the only time he had a big game for the Cubs because, man, that guy could really hit. One time he had a three homer game and I asked him, *"Billy, how quickly can you pick up the rotation of the pitch, whether or not it's gonna be a fast ball or breaking pitch?"* He said he could pick up the rotation when the ball was about three or four feet in front of him. Well, that doesn't give you an awful lot of time to adjust, but he could react that fast. That was amazing to me.

Billy was a very competitive player, and it probably ate him up that he never made it to the post-season with the Cubs, though he did make it to the playoffs with the Oakland A's later in his career. But just like Ernie Banks, Ferguson Jenkins, and Ron Santo, he never played in a World Series.

Williams' career started in 1959 when he played in just a few games, and he finally made it up to the big leagues, full time, in 1961. He won the Rookie of the Year that year and went on to set a National League record for consecutive games played with 1,117 between 1962 and 1971. Steve Garvey broke the record in the late

70s and early 80s. Williams had thirteen straight seasons where he hit twenty or more home runs and drove in at least 84 runs, from 1961 to 1973. He had his best year in 1972 at age 34, amazingly, when he led the league with a .333 mark and also posted a .606 slugging percentage. He hit 37 home runs and drove in 122 runs, and finished behind Johnny Bench in the MVP voting, just as he had done in 1970. The next year he was traded to the A's, where he helped lead them to the 1975 American League West championship as a designated hitter. They lost to the Boston Red Sox in the play-offs, who eventually lost to the Big Red Machine—the Cincinnati Reds—in the World Series.

Williams finished his career with a lifetime .290 batting average, 426 home runs and 1475 runs batted in. He was elected to the Hall of Fame in 1987, and on August 13th of that same year, had his number 26 retired at Wrigley Field. In 1999, Billy was named as a finalist to the Major League Baseball All-Century Team. Billy was a real laid back guy, and really easy to talk to.

The next game I pitched in was against the Chicago White Sox in the fifth annual Boys Baseball Benefit game. A crowd of nearly 24,000, the largest paid attendance of the year in Comiskey Park, watched six White Sox pitchers blank our hitters on six hits, never permitting one runner past second base. I pitched the last six innings of the game and Tommy Davis scored the only run, when he singled, stole second, and took third on a wild pitch and came home when second baseman Lee Elia dropped a pop fly hit by Sandy Alomar. Even though the game didn't count, I was pleased with my performance. Durocher told me as we were leaving the clubhouse that I had really impressed him with my control and ability to work ahead of the hitters. I felt like he was starting to believe in me, and it was a good feeling.

I pitched, in relief, in the first game of a doubleheader on July 17th. It was my last relief appearance of the season, though I didn't know it at the time. The team was on a winning streak (4 straight) and had a chance to move into fifth place by the end of the day. Ernie Banks, who loved to play two, of course, had a great first game. He was 37, but could still get his bat going now and again. "As I got more mature," Banks said after the game, "I have not been a good hitter with two strikes against me as I used to be. I used to feel like I was a good two-strike hitter when I was younger." But he was that day. He slammed a three-run home run in the first inning. Then, after our starter, Bill Hands, had given all three back, Banks hit a two-run dinger in the fifth, and that was all we needed. We won 8-4, and Banks drove in 6 runs.

I'll never forget this game because while I was walking to the mound I tripped and fell, and lost my composure. I entered the game in the eighth and walked the first batter. Again, Durocher didn't have the patience to let me wiggle my way out of it and he immediately brought in Regan. Unfortunately, we lost the second game of the doubleheader, 8-0, and that ended our five game streak. It also dropped the team back into sixth place.

Back to the Minors

Durocher wasn't using me very much in the majors and the Cubs organization began to feel like I'd be better served by pitching more innings. They sent me back to Triple-A in early August so I could pitch regularly for Tacoma. I was disappointed, but I also knew that I really did need to pitch more. I figured I'd be back up in the majors, and I'd be there for good soon enough.

As it turned out, the Cubs needed me one more time that season, and soon I would get my first start in the big leagues.

Chapter 7

Up Again

❖❖

Tacoma was in fifth place when I was sent back to the minors, and only a game away from being dead last, so the team really needed an infusion of good pitching. I was glad I'd be able to help. I know it sounds funny to say I was happy to be sent back to the minors, but in some ways, I was. I just wasn't getting to pitch enough with the big club, and I knew I couldn't be effective pitching every fourth or fifth game, and then pitching maybe one inning—if I was lucky. At that point, I figured I was going to have a long major league career, anyway, and I figured honing my skills for a few months in the minors could only help. I was very excited about 1969. Even though I only had a brief stint in the major leagues in '68, I pitched well enough to know that I belonged.

We knew we had a good team in 1968, and that we'd be even better in '69. We had quite a few good pitchers, such as Ken Holtzman, Joe Niekro, Ferguson Jenkins, Rich Nye and Bill Hands.

I knew it was going to be difficult for me to break into that rotation, but I also figured I had good enough stuff that they'd find a way to use me—maybe they'd make me a lefty specialist. I even thought I had a chance to make it as the fifth starter, or as a long reliever. I wanted to make that 1969 team and help them win the pennant.

When I left Chicago, I flew to Seattle just before the team left for a three game series with the Spokane Indians. JoAnn was left in Chicago with the task of packing, cleaning out our apartment, and getting ready to fly back home. She stayed with her parents in Olympia because there was only a month left in the season and I was pretty sure I would be called up again to play for Chicago. We had mixed feelings about being home because we enjoyed our time with family and friends, but I wanted to be back in Chicago pitching in the major leagues.

Ken Holtzman was a guy I admired from a distance. He had a great 15-year career and I really enjoyed watching him work. He attended the University of Illinois and was selected by the Cubs in the 1965 amateur draft. He pitched only twelve games in the minor leagues in 1965, going 8-3 with a 1.99 earned run average, which was pretty impressive. He broke in with the Cubs with three relief appearances, and became a member of the starting rotation in 1966, when he went 11-16 as a rookie. That team came in last, but they were competitive every year for the next five.

Many people called Ken the new Sandy Koufax, because he was a young, Jewish pitcher. Of course, that wasn't fair. It was impossible to live up to that, although Ken did beat the veteran in their only meeting, on September 25th, 1966, 2-1, taking a no-hitter into the ninth. Koufax retired after that season.

In 1967, Holtzman spent a lot of time away from the team in the National Guard, fulfilling his military obligation. That was very common in the late 60s. In 1967, Ken pitched in only 12 games, and was a perfect 9-0. After that, he became a regular with the Cubs and a very good number two starter behind Ferguson Jenkins. He went 11-14 in 1968, and then posted back-to-back 17-win seasons. He pitched his first no-hitter on August 19, 1969 at Wrigley Field against the Atlanta Braves, who went on to win the division that year. Ron Santo hit a 3-run homer and the Cubs won 3-0, beating Phil Niekro. Amazingly, Ken didn't strike out a single batter! It was the first no-hitter ever thrown by a left-handed pitcher at Wrigley Field. Hank Aaron almost broke up the no-hitter with a blast in the seventh inning, but luckily for Holtzman, the wind was howling that day and it blew the ball back into the park. Billy Williams leaped up and caught the ball against the vines.

Holtzman faced Aaron again in the ninth and got him to ground out to complete the no-hitter. In 1970 Holtzman had his best year with the Cubs, with a 17-11 record and a 3.38 ERA. He finished fifth in the National League in strikeouts (202) and innings pitched (287 2/3), third in starts (38), sixth in complete games, and ninth in wins.

I wanted to be ready to make a real difference for the Cubs next time I got called up to the major leagues, so I really wanted to pitch well for Tacoma. Whitey Lockman, our manager, approached me before my first start and said, *"Darcy, I want you to pitch every game like it's going to be your last one here—you could be called back up to the majors at any time."* The other players on the team treated me differently this time around. Having played in the majors gave me a new respect with my teammates, and they were counting on me to help get the team turned around.

It felt good to be a starting pitcher again. The Spokane Indians were the top affiliate of the Los Angeles Dodgers. I got off to a little bit of a shaky start, giving up a run in the first inning on a couple of hits, but I settled down after that. In the sixth inning, with two outs and the bases empty, I got my first hit of the game, a single. The Cubs knew I could hit—I'd originally been drafted by the Yankees as a first baseman—and later on that season Lockman would use me as a pinch hitter. That was the first hit of the game for our club, and it looked like we might lose a heart breaker. In the eighth, however, we exploded for eight runs and blew it wide open. Funny how that can happen in baseball. With one out and a man on, I laced a single to right. That chased the Spokane pitcher, Leon Everett, who had owned the Tacoma Cubs that year. After a walk, we just started banging out single after single, and it became a conga line across home plate for us. Lockman lifted me after 7 1/3 innnings—it was over 90 degrees that day and I was starting to tire. I'd also only pitched 16 innings in the major leagues, so it was understandable that he didn't want to stretch me out my first time back.

Lockman was pleased and after the game, and said, *"We gained a certain amount of self respect tonight because this was the first time in 27 innings that we scored some earned runs against the Indians' pitcher, Leon Everett, this season.*" He also kidded me after the game and said to me, "*I don't know if I'm more pleased with your pitching or your hitting.*"

My next start was against the Vancouver Mounties. A major league scout attending the game admitted he'd missed the boat when it came to evaluating my potential a few years back. In the paper, Babe Barberis, a longtime Pacific Northwest scout for the Pittsburgh Pirates said, "I couldn't see the boy as a pitcher when he was playing for North Thurston High prior to his graduation in 1965." He also said that he thought the Yankees should have offered me a better contract. "Obviously, [Eddie] Taylor wasn't much more impressed with the kid than I was, since the Yankees refused to offer him enough to make him interested in signing a professional contract." But the Yankees' contract had nothing to do with my decision to go to college—I liked the contract they offered me. I'd reached a point in my life where I knew I needed to get a college education in order to start figuring things out. If the Yankees had allowed me to stay in school, maybe my career would have been a lot different.

I struggled in the first inning against the Mounties—it was becoming a trend, but this time I managed to keep the opposition from scoring. In the first, I walked Tony LaRussa. Yes, *that* Tony LaRussa, who has since gone on to have a long career as the major league manager of the Oakland A's and St. Louis Cardinals. He was playing second base in that game. I walked the second batter, too, and then uncorked a wild pitch that let both players advance a base. I decided to calm myself down after that. I dug in and managed to get the next two batters to pop up to the infield. The last hitter fouled off a few pitches before grounding out feebly. I put it in cruise control after that.

"We let him off the hook in the first inning, and he never gave us a chance after that," Vancouver manager Mickey Vernon said after the game.

I went on to pitch a complete game shut out and didn't allow another batter to reach third base. Barberis said, *"After watching the boy turn in this brilliant job, I'm sure Taylor would like to be able to turn back the clock by a couple of years."*

Another interested observer in the stands that day, Dwight "Red" Adams, a former Pacific Coast League pitching star and a scout for the Dodgers, said, *"He simply overpowered the left-handed hitters with that hard curve, and he threw his fastball past the right-handed batters."*

Reading these things in the paper made me think about Fred Martin, and I felt grateful that I had gotten the chance to work with him at Lodi. Without his coaching, I would not have been nearly as effective.

The team was starting to play better—we won three of four from Vancouver—and though we didn't have much of a chance to catch the first place Spokane Indians, we wanted to see just how high we could climb—we focused on winning as many games as possible, and moving past the Portland Beavers in the standings to fourth place. We had eleven games left with them. There was a lot of buzz about my pitching in the papers. They raved about me and Archie Reynolds, an up and coming right-handed pitcher. We were rated then as the two most promising pitchers in the Cubs' farm system. Reynolds went on to have a short career with the Cubs, pitching in short spurts over five seasons.

The newspaper started running stories about me. In the News Tribune, they said,

"Rookie southpaw Darcy Fast, the pitching pride of neighboring Lacey who is being hailed as the most exciting newcomer to Pacific Coast League baseball this season, will take the mound for Tacoma in this Saturday night's second game of the current Cheney Stadium series with Portland. The 21-year old lefty is coming off a three-hit, 2-0 victory over the Vancouver Mounties earlier in the week. Gary Boyd, a rangy right-hander who joined the Beavers within the fortnight after completing a six-month service hitch, will handle the Portland serving in the 7:45 p.m. engagement. The series will be concluded with a Sunday afternoon double-header, starting at 1:30 p.m."

I was concentrating on my pitching career at that point, and nothing else. If someone had walked up to me and told me that someday in the not-too-distant future I'd become a minister, I'd have said they were crazy. I was thinking about getting back to the major leagues in 1969 and not much else. JoAnn and I would sometimes talk about it, and imagine the long, successful career I d have.

The four game set with the Beavers did not get off to a good start, and unfortunately that first game would set the tone for the rest of the series. We lost 7-6 in 15 innings. We had a 6-2 lead entering the ninth, but Portland pushed across four runs in the last inning to tie the score. Bobby Tiefenauer, our knuckle-ball reliever, was charged with all four runs, though perhaps there was a good reason why he didn't have it that night—he'd pitched 4 2/3 innings of relief two days before, helping us hold onto our final win against Vancouver. Tiefenauer was actually at the end of a ten year major league career. He was struggling to make it back, which he did one last time. He pitched about thirteen innings for the big club in 1968, before retiring to become a coach, both in the majors and minors, for the Phillies.

I had a bout of wildness in the first inning, and this time it cost us. After striking out the lead off hitter, I walked the number two and three batters in their lineup. I struck out Lou Piniella. The same Lou Piniella who became Rookie of the Year with the Kansas City Royals and went on to manage the Yankees, Reds, Mariners and the Chicago Cubs. When I struck him out, both runners took off and our catcher, John Boccabella, threw wildly to third, allowing a run to cross. Then I flung a wild pitch up there that brought in a second run. I settled down after that, giving up only two more runs over the remaining eight innings, but we'd given them too much, and we went down 4-3. I still felt good about my performance, though, because I'd thrown a complete game and kept it close.

I lost my next couple of starts, and though I didn't dominate as I'd been doing, I still pitched fairly well, except against the Hawaiian Islanders. I lasted only four innings, giving up five runs (four earned) and walking two. Our club started well and took a quick lead on back-to-back home runs by Clarence Jones and John Boccabella. I wiggled out of trouble in the first with a double play and got the first two batters in the second, but then gave up a single and a walk. I threw a wild pitch, allowing both runners to move up, and then yielded a single to allow both to score. I was angry with myself, and Whitey Lockman tried to calm me down. He walked out to the mound said, *"Hey, it's just another game. The only good thing you can do is to get the next batter out."* It was no use, though. I walked the lead off batter to start the fifth, and then threw the ball past our first baseman fielding a sacrifice.

Before my next start, Whitey Lockman pulled me aside. *"Darcy,"* he said. *"You're being called up to the major leagues right after you pitch tonight."* That was great news! Unfortunately, I had a lot of trouble concentrating that night against the Seattle Angels. Whitely was a great manager, but I wish he would have told me about the call up after the game. We were winning 3-1 going into the seventh. I hit a single up the middle off Jim Bouton, the infamous author of Ball Four, in the sixth inning to score Mike White, but in the seventh inning I walked the lead off batter, but got the next hitter swinging, and figured I would keep mowing 'em down. But then I gave up a single, and the next guy hit a squibbler that could have turned into an inning ending double play, only our second baseman couldn't get a grip on the ball and it went for an infield hit, loading the bases. I then walked their pitcher, forcing in a run. I struggled with my control and, for some reason, I couldn't find my balance point at the worst possible time.

To make matters worse, when the next batter got up, I balked, forcing in the tying run. I'd never done that before in my career, but I'd let my concentration wane after giving up the walk to the opposing pitcher. I knew better than to let my concentration drift like that, but it happened. The next batter hit a sacrifice fly and we ended up losing the game 4-3. I was still confident, though, and knew that I was getting guys out consistently. It would take more than a lousy balk to mess with my confidence. After the game I gathered my equipment and took the next plane out of Seattle to meet the Cubs in Los Angeles.

Playing at Chavez Ravine

It was August 28th, 1968, and we were playing the Dodgers in a twilight doubleheader at Chavez Ravine, the large and beautiful 56,000 seat stadium in Los Angeles. Walter O'Malley, the Dodger's owner, had moved the team from Brooklyn to Los Angeles in 1957 under much heart break from the loyal Dodger fans. Ebbets Field had been the home of the Dodgers since 1938, and they had won their only World Series while tenants at Ebbets Field in 1955. The fans did not want the team moved, but O'Malley felt the stadium seating was too small and that there weren't enough parking spaces, so he began looking for another location. To his credit, he did not want the team moved from Brooklyn, but when he lobbied for a dome stadium for his Dodgers at Atlantic Yards in Brooklyn, the New York Building Commissioner Robert Moss insisted the new site be at Flushing Meadow, the site of the current Shea Stadium. This conflict resulted in O'Malley looking to the potential in Los Angeles, and the Dodgers moved there after the 1957 season, while the New York Giants, their long-time rivals, moved to San Francisco.

Chicago had called me up to pitch the second game of the twilight double-header against the Dodgers. Many celebrities from came out for the game, because they were going to play a celebrity softball game in between the two big league matches. They were raising money for charity. Jackie Gleason was there — he was a good friend of Leo Durocher's, and we talked briefly before the game in the visiting team clubhouse.

The day before I was scheduled to pitch, our pitching coach Pete Reiser grabbed me in the locker room and told me stay at the hotel during the first game of the double header. Durocher had given him specific instructions: *"Don't have Fast come to the first game. Just have him come out to the second game."* He didn't want me sitting around, getting nervous.

Staying at the hotel was just as nerve wracking as watching the game would have been. In fact, it was pretty lonely after everyone else boarded the team bus, and I think I would have enjoyed the distraction of another game to keep me company. I paced back and forth in my room and watched part of the game on TV. Finally, I decided to head to the stadium. I took a yellow cab from the hotel and the cabbie had the game on. We were winning the game after exploding for six runs in the top of the first inning. Phil Regan pitched the last three innings and sealed the win for Rich Nye.

When I first stepped onto the field, I couldn't believe how many people there were in the stands. The place was packed. I walked out to the bullpen and started warming up about 20 minutes before the second game started and I was looking forward to pitching a great game.

Don Kessinger led off the game with a single and Glenn Beckert followed with a double. Kessinger scored on a ground out and Beckert on a sacrifice fly, and just like that, we had a 2-0 lead. The team had been playing better and had moved up to fourth place in the standings, though we were still fifteen games behind the front-running Cardinals.

My heart was pounding when I took the mound, so I settled myself down by thinking about all the success I'd already had in my career. It was really a blessing to me that I got to pitch at all in the majors. This thought must have helped, because I got off to a blazing start. After a ground out, I struck out the next two batters. In the second, I surrendered a home run to the Dodgers' right fielder, Len Gabrielson, but I didn't give up any other hits. In the top of the third, Beckert scored after walking on a Ron Santo double to right, and we had a

3-1 lead. At that point, I thought I was settling into a nice rhythm in the game, and it felt like I was in command. In the fourth, however, I ran into a little trouble. I walked the first two batters, but then I struck out the next batter and thought I might get out of it. I gave up a single, and then another walk. Durocher came storming out of the dugout. He didn't even allow the pitching coach, Pete Reiser, to talk to me. He just came out himself and asked for the ball.

Durocher always did things very dramatically, which sometimes took away from the game. It was kind of like a sitcom sometimes — *"The Leo Durocher Show."* For example, in 1969, he decided to get married and left the team for three days during the middle of a pennant race. Mr. Wrigley found out about it and almost fired Leo.

I saw him coming out to the mound to pull me and I started getting a bit angry: I still had a lot of pitches left and I wanted to win or lose the game on my own. I really felt like Durocher should have left me in there. Even Rich Nye told me afterwards that Leo had pulled me too quickly. I guess no pitcher likes to get yanked. In the eighth, Hands gave up a couple of hits and Durocher brought in Regan yet again. Poor Phil Regan. All those innings he was pitching would come back to haunt him and the Cubs toward the end of the 1969 season. He immediately gave up a double, and before we knew it the Dodgers had thrown up six quick runs. We ended up losing 8-4.

Baseball Chapel

In 1968, there happened to be a few guys on the team that had a strong Christian faith, and I found that really encouraging. One of them was Randy Hundley, our catcher, and also Don Kessinger, our shortstop. Those two guys were responsible for helping to start a Baseball Chapel in the majors. When players were on the road, it was nearly impossible to go to Sunday services, so Hundley and Kessinger got pastors and Christian athletes to come to our motel on Sundays and speak to us.

It was nice knowing that there were other guys with a strong faith in the big leagues, and that they weren't afraid to say so in public, either. Fran Tarkenton, the great Minnesota Vikings and New York Giants quarterback, spoke one Sunday morning at our baseball chapel in Philadelphia, and most of the team attended. I remember meeting in a conference room of the Marriot Motor Inn and Fran talked about his faith in Christ and how he was raised in a Christian home. He shared some of the struggles and challenges he faced as a professional athlete and how God had helped him in his life. I remember he said that, as a Christian, he wasn't perfect. He said he still made mistakes, but he knew that God's love for him did not change depending how "good" he was. He said his motivation wasn't based on what other people think, but on what God wanted for his life. He said, "My greatest desire is to honor God in every-thing I do—as a father, husband and professional football player." I was really impressed with his story, and so were some of the other players. Several players made a commitment to accept Jesus Christ that day.

Little did I know what Baseball Chapel would become today: an international ministry recognized by Major and Minor League Baseball and responsible for the appointment and oversight of all team chapel leaders—over 400 throughout professional baseball. Their ministry is directed toward players, coaches, managers, baseball wives, umpires, and the front office and ballpark staff.

Baseball Chapel's ministry extends throughout Major and Minor League Baseball, and reaches outside the United States, serving leagues in Mexico, Puerto Rico, Venezuela, the Dominican Republic, Nicaragua, and Japan.

In 1973, Watson Spoelstra contacted Commissioner Bowie Kuhn with the idea of organizing a chapel program for every major league team. Kuhn granted approval and Baseball Chapel was created. In 1974, services were switched from hotels to ballparks, and chapels were first held during the playoffs. Baseball Chapel is a non-denominational Christian ministry committed to the spiritual development of people throughout pro baseball.

Today some of the greatest players are active in Baseball Chapel, and have publicly shared their testimonies:

Garret Anderson, Outfielder - Anaheim Angels

"The 2002 World Series was a tremendous experience for everyone involved. But as great as it was to be fan, it's completely different to be on the team. It's one thing to know about the Angels

and another thing to actually be a member of the Anaheim Angels team.

For many years, my life was like the difference between being a fan and actually being a part of the team. I grew up knowing about God, but I really didn't know Him. Yes, I went to church, stayed out of trouble and tried to live a good life. But it wasn't until a couple of years ago that I recognized and understood that Jesus died for me because I am a sinner. It was then that I surrendered my life to Him, trusting in what He did for me—not what I could do for myself to earn a place in heaven. The Bible states, "For by grace you have been saved by faith; and that not of yourselves, it is the will of God; not as a result of works, that no one should boast." (Ephesians 2:8-9)

Over the past few years I've grown to know Christ in a deeper way through reading His Word, the Bible. He has guided me through the challenges of being a husband, father and major league baseball player. He has enabled me to lean on Him and make wise decisions. I have experienced the awesome power of prayer and witnessed God's amazing love in so many ways. In the everyday pressures of life, I have learned that God's promises are true. My favorite scripture verse is from Proverbs: "A gentle answer turns away wrath." (Proverbs 15:1)."

Carlos Beltran, Outfielder - New York Mets

"When I was in Kansas City, everything was going well for me. My marriage was good and I was very successful in baseball, but

something was missing in my life. That something was Christ. Every human being is born with a little defect in his heart. That defect is a hole in the heart that can only be filled by Jesus Christ. One night at a Bible Study in a Kansas City hotel room after a home game, the hole in my heart was filled. Accepting Jesus Christ into my heart was the biggest decision that I ever made. I'd been feeling like I wanted to have a better life, and I found it in God. It's not that everything is perfect now or that I don't have struggles anymore. But it's been easier going through it with Christ. God continues to change me everyday. Little by little He is taking away the things that He doesn't want me to do. What was important to me before is no longer important because I found a better life in God.

That night in Kansas City, I understood that we are all sinners. We can however, be forgiven for our sins because of Jesus Christ's payment for our sins on the cross. "But God showed His love for us in that while we were still sinners, Christ died for us." (Romans 5:8). When I die, I know that I'm going to heaven because I accepted Christ and He lives in me. I believe, because I'm saved, that I'm going to spend eternity with Him. God loves you, too, and He wants you to accept Jesus into your heart. Don't be afraid. Simply trust Him."

Jason Schmidt, Pitcher - Los Angeles Dodgers

"My mother lost a battle with brain cancer in April 2003. This was very tough time for me, and surprisingly, the most inspiring moment of my life. At her funeral, everyone that spoke mentioned

how she made a life-altering impact on them. She left a legacy that directed them to Jesus Christ. She made an impact in their day-to-day life, and more importantly, on their eternity.

How do you want to be remembered? What is your purpose? These are the questions I asked myself, and questions that I now ask you. I found that my purpose in life was to glorify God in my daily life by being the man He wants me to be, while trying to make a positive impact on others. This all begins with a personal relationship with Jesus Christ. You can have this purpose and direction too."

<u>*Mike Sweeney, First Baseman - Kansas City Royals*</u>

"My Dad put a baseball in my hand when I was three years old and that started me on a path that has resulted in the privilege of playing in the major leagues. In addition to nurturing my interest in baseball, my parents set a Godly example in our home. They laid a foundation for my own personal faith in Jesus Christ, which took on a deeper meaning when I was 14 years old. It was then I became fully committed to Him. He was now my Lord, my Savior, and my best friend.

Facing the ups and downs that come with being a major league ballplayer, I can experience contentment regardless of my circumstances and joy in knowing that God has a purpose for my life. How awesome it is knowing that God loves me so much that He was willing to leave heaven and die on a cross to pay for my sins. Realizing that eternal life is by God's grace, not something I can earn by doing good things, is what makes it possible to have an intimate, personal relationship with Him.

Love for baseball and for God have been passions of mine since I was young. However, the best I can ever accomplish in baseball can only bring temporary happiness to my life, while knowing Christ brings me eternal joy."

Lyle Overbay, First Baseman - Tornoto Blue Jays

"I didn't grow up going to church, so I didn't know much about the Bible and what it had to offer. Even then, God was always working in my life—I just didn't know it. Again, through trials and errors, God put me in front of my wife, knowing she would be able to show me the gift God has given all of us—His Son, Jesus Christ. Sarah and I vowed to commit ourselves to go to church in order to give our boys what we didn't have at an early age, and that was God.

God gave me the gift to play baseball, which ultimately brought me closer to him by guiding me to Baseball Chapel. Baseball Chapel provides Minor and Major League teams with a pastor leading a Bible study on Sunday, whether we are home or on the road. For me, Baseball Chapel was the first place I really came to learn what Christianity was all about. Close friends that God put in front of me challenged me to grow closer to Him and grow to better understand the gifts God has given me. Eventually it all comes down to one of my favorite Bible verses: Matthew 19:26. Jesus said, "With man this is impossible, but with God all things are possible." God sent his only Son to earth to die on the cross for all of our sins and we must accept that we are far from perfect and need God in our lives.

Ironically, accepting the Lord Jesus Christ into my life was one of the easiest things that I have ever done. Bible studies, Christian parenting classes, and Baseball Chapel are just some of the ways I am committing myself to serve the Lord Jesus Christ."

These major league baseball players have accepted God's gift that has been made available to everyone. That gift is Jesus Christ. Once you receive that gift, you will never want to return it, and you will never be the same! The Apostle Paul, when thinking about the gift that was given to him, said, *"Thanks be to God for his indescribable gift!" (2 Corinthians 9:15)* Paul was one of the best communicators of all time, yet he could only say, *"I don't have the words to describe Him. All I can do is thank God for His inexpressible gift."*

Some people try to earn God's gift, but then it's not a gift—it's simply exchange for your work. The Bible says, *"For it is by grace you have been saved, through faith—and this is not from yourselves, it is the gift of God—not by works, so that no one can boast." (Ephesians 2:8-9)* Other people try to earn God's gift, but we can't buy it either. The gift of salvation is not for sale because the price has already been paid through the death of Jesus Christ.

Years ago the Chicago Cubs were facing the New York Giants in (September of 1908) the Polo Grounds. The Polo Grounds was, as the name suggests, built for the sport of polo. It was noted for its distinctive bathtub shape, with very short distances to the left and right field walls, but an unusually deep center field.

The pennant was on the line. Every game was important. In the bottom of the 9th inning, the Giants had base runners on first and third with the scored tied 1-1.

Fred Merkle, a young 19 year-old rookie, was the Giants' runner on first base. The next batter hit a line-drive single and the runner from third base came home for the Giants' victory. They had taken the lead in the pennant chase and their fans swarmed the field. Merkle was bewildered as the crowd swarmed onto the field, and he stopped running. Thinking the game was over, he ran off the field. But he had forgotten an important rule of baseball—he did not touch second base. The Cubs retrieved the ball and touched second for the out.

The game was declared a tie by the umpires because order could not be restored and because the fans would not leave the playing field. The Giants and the Cubs went on to finish the season and tied for the pennant. They now had to play a one-game playoff. The Cubs won the game, and went on to win their only World Series in the history of the franchise.

Fred Merkle was never forgiven by the New York Giants for that blunder. He went on to have a solid career of 14 years and a lifetime average of 273. However, everywhere he went, he was reminded by baseball fans of his mental error—his terrible mistake made on but one day of his rookie season.

Unlike many people, Jesus offers complete forgiveness to you for every mistake—every sin you've ever committed. When you accept what Jesus did for you on the Cross, when He died in your place, paying the full penalty for your sins, you become a Christian. Jesus has exchanged His life for yours?

The gift of Jesus Christ is free, but it's not cheap. It cost God the death of his one-and-only Son. Salvation is available to any and everyone who wants it. John 1:12 sums up the ultimate choice that we must make: *"Yet to all who received him, to those who believed in his name, he gave the right to become children of God."*

To "receive" Christ means to welcome him as an honored guest and to have him make your heart his home. Jesus said, *"Here I am! I stand at the door and knock. If anyone hears my voice and opens the door, I will come in and eat with him, and he with me." (Revelation 3:20)*

You will never truly experience all that life is intended to be until you receive God's gift to you. If you've never received Jesus Christ, don't leave the gift of God's grace unopened. Invite Jesus Christ into your heart.

Chapter 8

My Dog Ate My Homework

Every Cubs fan worth his weight in sports history knows what happened to the team in 1969 — it's probably the season people think of most when they think "Cubs" — so I won't spend a lot of time recounting every painful detail. I will, however, drudge up a few unpleasant memories. On August 15th, 1969, the Cubs were 74 and 43, not to mention a 13.5 game cushion on the New York Mets (and a 9 game lead on the Cardinals). On September 1st, that lead was down to 4.5 games on New York, and by September 11th, the team found itself looking up in the standing at the Metropolitans. Much has been written about that team's unfortunate collapse, and some of it true.

It's fair to say that a few of the bigger names faded down the stretch during that year. Ernie Banks, most famously, hit only .186 in September with one home run, and Leo Durocher, who wasn't much for taking responsibility himself, often blamed Banks for the collapse. But Ernie was 38 at the time and had bum knees, so there was no way he should have been getting over 600 at-bats in a season, and that's why he started breaking down toward the end. How could he not? Leo should have been resting him a lot more than he was, in my opinion. Don Kessinger also faded in September, hitting only .223. Ron Santo, Randy Hundley and Glenn Beckert slumped down the stretch as well. Hundley was hurting; everyone knew that. He was the best catcher on the team, so Leo kept running him out there—he finished the season catching in 151 games, which by today's standards is miraculous. Although the others did slump some down the stretch, it was probably inevitable, and it wasn't the primary reason the team lost 27 of 45 from August 15th to the end of the year. Kessinger was having the best year of his career, and if he'd kept it up, he would have put up numbers that far and away exceeded his normal season, so a little fade was sort of inevitable there. He still ended up having a heck of a year. The same was true of Santo and Hundley—they ended up having normal years when you look at the final numbers.

No, it wasn't the regulars. I think most Cubs fans understand that. What hurt the team more than anything, I believe, was a lack of pitching depth, especially in the dog days of summer. Relievers Phil Regan and Rich Nye had pitched a lot of innings over two seasons, and there was no way they could keep up the pace. The starters, Jenkins, Hands, and Holtzman, had to try to eat up the innings to compensate, and they began to tire, too. In other words, by the end of 1969, the team was playing as if it were missing one or two important cogs in the machine. The team needed one more reliever, or a starter to occasionally eat up some innings. I could have been that player—only fate got in the way.

Back in college, I had trouble keeping my focus because I was looking forward to the 1969 season so much. JoAnn and I spent a lot of time then planning our future together. I probably drove her a little crazy with all my talk about baseball, but it was hard to resist. I'd gone from collecting bubble gum cards to rubbing elbows with Ernie Banks and Billy Williams and playing against Hank Aaron and Willie Mays. What young player wouldn't start dreaming about striking out the last batter in the World Series, tossing his glove into the air and jumping into the arms of catcher Randy Hundley? I had dreams like that frequently, but I kept my focus. I wasn't going to get there without hard work, so I did my best to stay in shape that winter. Every day, after classes, I went to the C.C. Perry gym and worked out. I would get LeRoy Tucker or Dan Kaiser, and we would work out together. I knew these guys wanted me to make it big, and they were willing spend the time with me during the off-season to make it happen. When the weather in Portland was good, I'd pitch to them outside. When the weather was rainy and nasty, which was most of the time, we worked out together in the gym. I was doing everything I could physically to be ready for spring training in Scottsdale, when pitchers and catchers reported in February.

One day, something happened during the winter that nearly sent me to the hospital. Warner Pacific is located on Mt. Tabor, and in January, we had a terrific winter storm. Snow covered Portland, and the college campus was one sheet of ice. Several of us guys started clowning around one evening and we grabbed some plastic clothes baskets and headed down the hill. I had no idea how fast you can travel in a clothes basket going down Mt. Tabor, and I barely stopped before going out on 68th Street—a busy street below the college. I was thankful to be alive, let alone to still have the opportunity to play baseball.

I'll risk stating the obvious by mentioning that the late '60s were a turbulent time. The Vietnam War was in full swing, and it seemed there were protests, sometimes violent, every day. There were other signs of unrest, like the famous student protests in France in May '68, followed soon after by the assassination of presidential candidate Robert Kennedy. And there were amazing human triumphs, like the Apollo 11 moon landing. I watched in awe with the rest of the world on July 20th, as Neil Armstrong uttered his immortal phrase: "That's one small step for man, one giant leap for mankind."

And baseball—with its familiar, comfortable rhythms, and with its appearance each spring as a promise of rebirth—was as riveting to the American public as it ever was. 1969 was finally going to be *the* year—the first time the Cubs would win the World Series since the days of Tinker to Evers to Chance. The momentum had been building for a few years. The Cubs finished 87-74 in 1967, good enough for third place. Many fans thought that year was a huge success, because the team surpassed everyone's expectations—they'd finished dead last the year before, going 59-103. But the young players were starting to gel, and, more than anything, the pitching was really beginning to come around. Jenkins won 20 games and finished second in the league in strikeouts, and Holtzman, while limited to just 12 appearances because of the War, won 9 and lost none. Plus, rookies Rich Nye and Joe Niekro, both 22, combined for 375 innings and 23 wins. Everyone, players and fans alike, had high hopes for '69.

The main reason I can remember we finished in third all these years later is because when I went back to Warner Pacific after the '68 season, JoAnn and I unexpectedly received a check one day in the mail. It was our portion of the World Series money. Even though the Cubs had finished in third, the top three teams got a share of the series money. The check was for six or seven hundred bucks, but it was exciting at the time because we really needed it. We bought some groceries and paid for some of our college expenses, but I was especially happy because the Cubs had voted me a share of the money. This meant they recognized my contributions to the team.

The Cubs finished 84-78 in 1968, even though they struggled mightily in the early part of the year, and Nye and Niekro were still adjusting to the majors. The team had the best record in the league from mid July to the end of the season. Also on the plus side, Billy Williams finished the year with 30 home runs, fourth in the league, and Banks hit 32 dingers, good enough for third in the NL. Meanwhile, Glenn Beckert led the league in runs, and Ron Santo and Williams tied for second in RBI, with 98. Fergie won 20 games for the second straight year, and Bill Hands won 16 games. That was also the first year the team had Phil Regan, who they'd gotten in a trade with the Dodgers. He threw 127 innings out of the bullpen, and led the league in saves. He also won 10. The players and the fans knew, after languishing for years near the bottom of the league, that the Cubs were no fluke.

When it was time for spring training, I had one thing in mind— I'm going to make the Cubs. The first person I saw when I got out of the cab that spring was old Leo. We were staying at the Ramada Inn in Scottsdale and I was getting ready to check in.

"Darcy," Leo said. *"We're really counting on you this year."* That's all he needed to say. I was ready to impress them, and I already felt like the season would be much easier for me this time around, because all the players would already know me. The fans were also starting to get to know my name. Ed Honeywell wrote in the The Tacoma News Tribune,

"To name just three, Gary Ross, Joe Decker and Darcy Fast are all certain to receive considerable attention when Manager Leo Durocher makes a final evaluation of the talent at his disposal preparatory to selecting the 10-man staff he'll send into the 1969 chase."

The stars were aligned: the team was coming off a promising season, we had potential all-stars all around the field, plus one of the most formidable trio of pitchers in the league. I was ready to be the last piece of the puzzle.

The war

1969 was my last year of college. That meant my automatic military deferment was also ending. I didn't want to get drafted into the Vietnam War, but I also knew that if the war continued another year, I would have to fulfill my military obligation. When the Cubs sent my contract out on January 24th, 1969, I wrote John Holland, the general manager of the team, a letter asking him why they were not finding an opening for me in the National Guard. I thought they'd found openings for other ballplayers. He wrote back and told me that they were doing everything they could to get me into the National Guard; they'd even put my name on a waiting list for one of the Illinois National Guard units. He also said, *"Your name has been placed on a waiting list, and if nothing develops before then, we will try to do something else in your behalf. Of course, you can receive a 90 day deferment which will enable you to get most of the baseball season in. Also, Bobby Adams is trying to get something arranged for you at either Ft. Lewis or the Washington National Guard. As soon as he has some definite information, I will advise you."*

He sent me my 1969 contract and I'd asked for a little more money, because the amount was less than I thought JoAnn and I could make if we both taught school the following year. I was kind of naive at the time—clubs paid what they wanted to pay. There were no agents, and free agency didn't exist. Mr. Holland was probably amused by my request. He wrote: *"I would not attempt to compete with what both you and your wife may receive on teaching contracts. If she had the same potential as a Major League pitcher, we would sign her up also."* I was just a 22-year-old kid dealing with people who had been in baseball for years. Mr. Holland knew what he was doing.

I signed the contract. In order to make it to spring training, though, I had to gamble and take a leave of absence from Warner Pacific. But I needed to keep my enrollment, because if the draft board discovered I wasn't in school, I could be in trouble. I went to the registrar of the college and explained my decision, but made sure I could stay enrolled. I had to make certain I could take incompletes in the classes, and they allowed me to do this.

I went to spring training, and I did really well for the three weeks I was there. However, one game I remember vividly was not one of my better outings. We were playing against the Oakland A's, and Duroucher brought me into the game in the 4th inning. The A's finished in 2nd place in 1968 and were one of the best teams in the America League. Hall of Famer Reggie Jackson and Rick Monday were playing that day for the A's, and when they saw that I was having control problems, they wrapped their arms with towels and tape when they came to the plate. Everyone in their dugout and some people in the stands were getting a big laugh and I was a little intimidated by their joking around. I just tried to ignore it and went on pitched to them. I found out later that Duroucher told someone in our dugout that he would have been more pleased with me if I would have thrown right at their head.

It wasn't long into spring training that I was notified that by my draft board that if I didn't continue to make normal progress towards graduation in June they were going to reclassify me *immediately* to 1A, which meant I could be drafted. I had an S2, which was a student deferment. I had to go back to school.

I contacted Mr. Holland and Leo Durocher and the traveling secretary, Blake Cohen, and explained to them what had happened. They told me to go right back to college. Mr. Holland said, *"We want you to go back there, but we want you to also note that we're going to continue to work even harder to get you in the National Guard, and when we do, then we'll know we can use you and not jeopardize your eligibility with the draft."* That same day, I had an airline ticket from Arizona back to Portland, Oregon, and I was back in classes the next day. I completed my student teaching at David Douglas High School in Portland, Oregon, finishing another eighteen hours. It was a hectic time.

Even though I was so busy trying to finish up the requirements for my degree, I still couldn't understand why I hadn't heard from the Cubs regarding my military situation. I heard later that Mr. Holland really wanted me to stay at spring training and not return to school. But when the college semester ended, the Cubs still hadn't found me an opening in the reserves or National Guard. I felt a lot of stress during this whole time, because it's difficult to come that close to your dream, so close you can kick it, only to see it snatched away. I really thought I could help the 1969 Cubs. What hurt me was that while I was doing so well, the only thing that prevented me from getting called up to the Major Leagues was my military obligations.

On July 14th, I wrote a letter to Mr. Holland. I was pretty disappointed and, looking back, I think I was just frustrated and needed a way to let it out:

"When I left spring training this year to go back to college I was under the impression that you were going to do everything possible to try and find an opening for me in an Army Reserve or National Guard Unit. You seemed so certain that an opening was available at that time, that I thought I would be able to come back to spring training in a matter of a few days. I haven't heard from you since regarding my military situation, but I do understand that you were able to find several other players openings during spring training.

It was an angry letter, and of course Mr. Holland and the Cubs weren't really at fault, but I was young and feeling very disappointed. I wrote,

If you had gotten me into a unit as you did these other ballplayers I would not have to miss any of the season and I may have been some help to the Cubs. I have worked hard to get myself in shape this season while at Tacoma and as of this letter I have a 5-1 record and a good ERA."

John Holland wrote back to me immediately. He wanted to make it clear that he'd done everything possible to get me in the service. He was a little miffed, too, at the tone of my letter.

"This will acknowledge your belligerent letter of July 14, 1969. Just to get the record straight regarding your military status, your school status and your contract with this organization, you came to me shortly after reporting to spring training informing us that you had been advised by your Draft Board that you had been reclassified to 1A for dropping out of school. You stated you felt you should return to school immediately and complete the semester <u>and</u> that you had applied to a National Guard Unit in Oregon and would be accepted around June 1st. I told you I agreed with your thinking regarding returning to school but in the mean time we would do everything we could to get you into a Reserve Unit. <u>That was done</u>. We applied to the Illinois National Guard for a space in one of their Units. Your name was placed on the list of a Unit that had the smallest waiting list of any Unit in Illinois. Unfortunately, they have not opened any of the Units in Illinois since last January and your name is still on that list. That is as much as we can do for anyone.

One player was accepted in Arizona, Joe Decker, whose name had been on their list for several months. I know of two other players in the Organization that have been accepted into a Reserve Unit in their home states, but they accomplished this strictly on their own. From the tone of your letter you seem to think they were given preferential treatment, which is the farthest thing from the truth. If we had that kind of influence with the Military we would certainly see that player Alexander was taken care of as we are losing him for two years next month.

Naturally, we are happy that you were able to get into an Oregon Unit as it is most difficult for a professional athlete since the Jo Jo White case in Basketball. Now as to your contract, the clause concerning pay during Military duty only covers weekend drills and two week summer camp drills or riot service during the season. We just confirmed this with Mr. Gaherin who represents management who in turn confirmed it with Mr. Miller who represents the Players Association. However, you can be thankful that you are with an Organization that goes beyond its contractual obligations especially to married men. I have instructed our Accounting Department to continue your salary to the end of the season. I can assure you that no other business or ball club would do this. Just check for yourself. Please advise us where the checks should be sent. Good luck and keep healthy."

Jo Jo White was one of the great basketball players in the late 60s and early 70s, and is perhaps best known for his role in a triple-overtime win over the Phoenix Suns in Game 5 of the 1976 NBA Finals. White was another one of the great Red Auerbach's "steals."

He was highly sought after in the 1969 NBA draft, but dropped to the Celtics because his two-year military obligation scared teams away. Somehow, though, he ended up in the Marine Reserve program and started playing right away. It became a touchy subject, because a lot of people said he was getting preferential treatment because he was an athlete. If you had influence and some pull during that time, you could get your name on the top of that list. It's what got George W. Bush in some hot water a few years back. But when it started becoming big news, in particular because of Jo Jo White, the Guard began to clamp down on it. Mr. Holland and the Cubs didn't want to have anything to do with that, understandably.

I thought it was generous of the Cubs to continue paying my salary, however. Players today are lucky that they don't have to get involved in issues like this.

Finally, after much worry, I was able to secure a spot for myself in the National Guard Unit in Oregon. I thought at the time that this made more sense than signing a teaching contract, because I thought the Unit would still leave me a chance to get called up. However, the National Guard didn't see it that way. They sent orders for me to report for active duty on July 28th for basic training. I went to the company commander of my National Guard unit and told him I was a professional baseball player, and asked him if there was any way that I could do my active duty after the season, in October. He said absolutely not. *"For us to give you any type of preferential treatment just wouldn't be fair,"* he said. That also meant I'd be in training for the rest of the summer, so my season with Chicago was definitely down the tubes. I reported to Tacoma, which was close to home, and began pitching for the Triple-A team while I waited to report for my military service.

I was still anxious to perform well in the minors, in spite of my disappointment. I was a little rusty when I got to Tacoma—I hadn't pitched in about a month—so they used me initially to pitch in relief in an attempt to whip me into shape. In my first start, I struggled through 6 and two-thirds of an inning, though I only gave up two earned runs, and struck out six to go along with five walks. Without time to practice, my control was a little shaky. I had a no decision in my next start, followed by another game where I struggled a little with my control. Things clicked into place, finally, toward the end of June, and I pitched what was probably my best game of the year.

It was Wednesday, June 25th, and I was facing the Hawaiian Islanders, the best hitting team in Triple-A at the time. Our club pushed across a single run in the second, with the help of back to back infield errors and a single. I gave up a towering home run to Hilario Rojas to lead off the sixth, and that was the last run either team allowed until the twelfth. I almost lost the game in the seventh when our centerfielder misjudged a fly ball. It tipped off his glove and went for a triple. But I got the next batter to ground out, and after an intentional walk, got the next on a punch out. We made two quick outs to begin the twelfth and it looked like we might be playing one of those games for the record books, but Roe Skidmore, our first baseman, lashed a double, and our catcher, Randy Bobb, followed that with a single and just like that, the game was over. In the end we won 2-1. Tacoma managed just four hits and Hawaii just seven. I walked three and struck out four.

Here's what Ed Honeywell, writing for The Tacoma News Tribune, had to say about the game the next day:

"In the light of Hawaii's 14-hit assault on Tacoma pitching Thursday night, plus the Islanders' 12-run output in a losing cause Tuesday and their 11-8 conquest Monday, Darcy Fast's superb Wednesday performance takes on added glitter... The Lacey lefty's 2-1 victory over Rickey Clark in a route-going, 12-inning gem was easily the standout mound job of the season registered by a Tacoma staff which has covered itself with distinction. What made Fast's effort so impressive was his excellent control—he issued only four walks and was seldom behind in the count all evening. Additionally, he grew steadily stronger as the game progressed, mowing down the enemy with consummate ease in closing stage. In the 12th, for instance, he effected the final three outs on just three pitches in locking the door on the Islanders."

My Dog Ate My Homework

I was frustrated that I wasn't going to get to play for the Chicago Cubs in 1969, but I was also extremely grateful that I'd landed an opening in the National Guard. I believe to this day it was divine providence.

I still hadn't heard from the Guard as of May, and I was starting to get pretty nervous. The way they recruited people for the National Guard and Reserve is a little random: when a spot opens up, they pull out a long list of hopefuls and just start calling people on the list. The first person to answer the phone gets the slot, so you just had to hope you were home when they called.

One night I was working on a term paper in human anatomy, which is the study of human movement. JoAnn and I left our apartment to go get dinner, and as I was locking the door, I heard what sounded like a paper being crumpled up. We had two small dogs, and I guessed what might be happening inside. I ran back into the apartment and there was Cocoa Bean, our little French, chocolate poodle, chewing on my paper like it was a steak. He'd jumped right onto the counter and didn't seem to mind that I'd come back—the paper must have been pretty tasty to him. I didn't have another copy, either, and I'm pretty sure no one would have believed that my dog ate my homework, so I raced over and started to pull the paper out of Cocoa Bean's mouth. Just then the phone rang.

I picked up and it was the first sergeant from the Salem National Guard calling to see whether or not I was available to join the Guard. They had one opening and he was calling to see if I wanted it. If JoAnn and I had left for dinner, I would have missed that telephone call and never gotten into the Guard. As funny as it was, I always felt it was a divine providence of God, because if Cocoa Bean hadn't found that kinesiology paper so delicious, I wouldn't have been back in the apartment to answer the phone call.

I was happy, of course, that I wasn't going to have to go to Vietnam. I knew guys who had given their lives over there—guys that I'd been in high school with who came back in a body bag. The United States lost over 60,000 men, and most of those were guys my age.

As far as baseball went, I had mixed feelings. I really thought '69 was going to be my breakout year with the Chicago Cubs. Tacoma ended up winning the Pacific Coast League championship, but I wasn't around to finish the season with them either. I didn't come close to finishing the season, in fact. I reported to Fort Ord on July 28th.

Fort Ord was a U.S. Army post covering about 20,000 acres on Monterey Bay in California. It was, as far as military bases go, not a horrible place. It was close to the beach and on most days the weather in California was beautiful, but sometimes even a nice place can be a nightmare. Everyone there knew that Fort Ord was a staging area for units heading off to the war, so if you were there, you probably were going to head straight overseas after training. The Fort was established in 1917 and served a few functions for the military over the years, until finally closing in 1994. Most of the land was given back to the state of California and is now the location for the Monterey Bay campus of California State University. Some of the space is also a nature preserve.

When I went through boot camp, I trained with the regular Army. There were only two of us in the National Guard in my company. The big difference was that I knew when I graduated from basic training, I was going home. The other guys were getting on an airplane heading straight to Vietnam. The drill sergeants and the other guys knew it, too, and it was not fun. They treated me differently, especially when they found out I was a professional baseball player. A lot of them thought, "Well, here's a pro ballplayer, he's got an easy life, somebody must have pulled a string for him."

I knew that wherever I was going to play ball from that point on, I would have to fly back to Salem, Oregon for monthly training, and then back. It wasn't just me, either. It was common then. We had seven players on that Pacific Coast League team that had military obligations. Guys were coming and going all the time. The same with the Chicago Cubs. Kessinger and Holtzman had military obligations, for example. It affected the season. You had to manage differently. Ken Holtzman was one of our best pitchers and Durocher had to build the rotation around his military schedule. The Guard members also had to train for two weeks during the summer, and they didn't care if it was a pennant or not—if you've got two weeks of summer camp, you had to leave the team. That was part of your National Guard duty.

Could I have Helped?

It's impossible now to say whether or not my presence on the 1969 Cubs would have made *the* difference. I can only look back at a few key moments in the season and wonder what could have been different if Durocher had been able to look out to his bullpen and see me warming up late in games. Phil Regan, Rich Nye, and even the starters would have gotten just a little more rest throughout the year, and maybe they would have been able to hold onto a few more leads. Or maybe I could have come out and struck out a few key lefties. In mid-September, the Cubs lost to the Cardinals 7-4, when they couldn't hold an eighth inning lead. Jenkins started the inning, and it was an exhausted Regan who allowed the winning runs to cross the plate. On September 15th, they lost to the Expos, a team that had already lost one-hundred games, when Dick Selma, Hank Aguirre, Ted Abernathy, and Rich Nye got beat around to the tune of an 8-2 loss. The bullpen lost another lead later in the week when rookie George Decker pitched well enough to win. That's the way it went for the Cubs all month.

But who's to say I would have helped in any one game down the stretch. Maybe just by eating up a few innings earlier in the year, filling in when needed, I could have spared Nye, Regan, Jenkins, Hands and Holtzman just a little wear and tear—those guys were exhausted both physically and mentally by the end of the season.

Or maybe nothing in the world could have helped. One thing that's often overlooked about that season is how good the Mets actually were. That squad is often referred to as "The Miracle Mets," but what they did only appeared miraculous because no one understood how good their players were. Any team that wins the World Series employing Hall of Fame pitchers Tom Seaver and Nolan Ryan is anything but miraculous. They turned out to be two of the best pitchers in the history of the game. The Mets began the season going just 21-23, but while the Cubbies went 8-17 in September, the Mets, behind Seaver and the rest of the young staff, won 38 of their last 49 games and ended up 100-62. They finished with a 2.99 ERA and led the league by tossing shutouts in 28 games. Seaver finished with a 25-7 record, while lefty Jerry Koosman went 17-9. That was a good team.

Chapter 9

The Upward Call

I was in the Oregon National Guard and no longer had to worry about the military draft, and I was done with college and ready to focus one-hundred percent on baseball. It was 1970, and after the disappointment of not being able to play in the majors because of my military training in 1969, I still felt like I could make my mark as a dominating lefty in the major leagues. I signed another contract and hoped the Cubs had big plans for me. Leo Durocher was interviewed during spring training about his ball players for the upcoming season and said he hadn't decided on who his fourth pitcher was going to be, but to bolster the bullpen he was very interested in Archie Reynolds, Joe Decker, and myself—especially after the way Phil Regan and Ted Abernathy tired late in the 1969 season. Here's what Omer Crone wrote in the Fresno Bee about it:

"Durocher is convinced he has more talent, more depth than a year ago. That is the old spring song, stale in October. Still, pro odds-makers rate the Cubs and Cardinals as co-favorites in the National League East, ahead of the world champion Mets. In a nutshell, Durocher—in matters of personnel—needs secondary pitching. Youngsters are being counted on to give Jenkins, Bill Hands and Ken Holtzman the support that was lacking last year on the starting line. 'I haven't decided on my fourth pitcher,' Durocher said, 'but it probably will be Jim Colburn... look at the kid throw the ball.' Colburn is a right hand fastballer from Tacoma, who pitched 15 innings for the Cubs for a 1-0 mark, after an excellent season with Tacoma, the Cubs' Triple-A club, champions of the Pacific Coast League. Archie Reynolds, Joe Decker and Darcy Fast, also up from Tacoma, and Dick LeMay, ex-Fresno Giant, are counted on to bolster a bullpen that got subpar work from Phil Regan and Ted Abernathy last season."

Even though Durocher said he was counting on Jim Colburn, I knew the number four spot in the rotation was wide open and I was determined to nail it down. I'd worked out all winter and was in the best shape of my life. Things started off well in spring training, too. I pitched against Oakland, San Francisco, and Cleveland, and I fared very well. It looked like I was going to be a lock for the team.

It turned out, though, that my major league career was snake-bit. I'd been bitten by a few metaphorical snakes during my years attempting to play pro ball, but the worst of it began that summer of 1970. For the first time in my career, I developed soreness in my shoulder. I felt it on a pitch in one spring training game. I didn't really know what to make of it, because I'd never had pain before in my arm, so I just kept throwing. I had pretty good control, but the velocity on my fast ball just wasn't there. I went out another day to pitch, but the pain got to be too much and I had to come clean with Durocher and our trainer. They decided to rest me for about a week. I probably should have been a little more nervous about it than I was, but since I'd never had arm trouble before, I just figured the pain would go away and I'd be back on track. I spent the week around the clubhouse, keeping my legs in shape and watching the other guys work out. It was the first arm problem I'd ever had, so they let me just kick back and take it easy. I started throwing lightly again in the bullpen, but my shoulder was still bothering me. They recommended that I have a cortisone shot. I'd never had one before, so I was a little worried. I spoke to our trainer, Al Scheuneman, and he said that other pitchers had the treatment and were fine after a short time. I got the cortisone shot, which made my arm feel better almost immediately, but I still had to wait a couple more weeks before I could throw again. I still wasn't that worried about it, and I certainly didn't feel like the end of my career was around the corner.

My shoulder trouble did ruin my chances of making the majors that season, however, and that was a little bit upsetting. You can't miss three weeks of spring training, especially when you're just coming up, and then pitch like you haven't missed a beat. It doesn't work that way. The Cubs sent me back to Tacoma to get myself straightened out, but Durocher told me he hoped to call me back up some time during the season. I was a little disappointed, but I couldn't blame them, since even I didn't know how my arm would react. I was just hoping to get another chance.

My first game with the Tacoma Cubs was on April 14th, 1970, against the Hawaiian Islanders. I didn't have my best control—I walked five—and my arm still felt a little sore, but I managed to get through almost 7 innings, giving up only four runs (two earned). Three double plays in the first three innings were about all that kept me from getting really hammered. Still, we were only trailing 3-2 entering the sixth inning, and our team rallied late and managed to squeeze out a 5-4 win. We entered the eighth down 4-3 after I'd given up a home run to Jarvis Tatum. But our centerfielder and leadoff hitter started a rally in the eighth with a single and stolen base. Jimmy McMath, our rightfielder, walked with a man on and two outs, and then John Hairston, our catcher, smacked a double to drive in two. Strangely, his hit was initially ruled a home run, but after the Hawaiian Islander's manager, Chuck Tanner, argued the call, it was changed. Our manager, Whitey Lockman, was livid. After the game he said, "Because Dale (the umpire) was closest, he shouldn't have asked for help from the other umpires, which he said he didn't. So it must have been Chuck Tanner's protest which caused him to change his decision." He paced back and forth in the locker room and was still angry hours after the game. If I'd gotten one more out I would have gotten the win, but that's the way things go in baseball sometimes: Reliever Dick LeMay got one out, but that was enough for the victory.

We were facing the Spokane Indians on April 23rd, and it was one of those April games that you tend to forget ever existed when you're playing under the blazing sun in the middle of July. It was cold, and the rain came and went as if someone was turning a faucet on and off for kicks. We played only five innings, though it took three and a half hours to get the game in. That was plenty on a day like that, and we ended up on the losing end of a 4-1 score. Spokane jumped out to a quick 1-0 lead when Dave Lopes started things with a double and Bob Valentine brought him in with a single. I settled down and we tied things in the second on a two-out rally—John Hairston hit a single, which was followed by Terry Hughes slashing a triple to right-center. It was wonderful watching him race around the bases and I thought we were going to build some momentum off of that. Naturally, the rains came and play was suspended for forty-four minutes. I got through the third, but my arm was sore when I came back in the fourth. I walked two, threw two wild pitches, and watched our shortstop miss a routine ground ball. They pushed across a run without even a hit! The fifth was worse. I had to wait through another long delay, this one thirty-three minutes, before getting out there again. My shoulder was tired and stiff, and I gave up a third hit to Lopes, two more walks, and tossed another wild pitch. After a stolen base and another error, we were down 4-1. The rains came again and the game was called. It was my second straight loss.

I was disappointed in myself, but I couldn't get my arm straightened out. I pitched in a total of four games that season, and none of them went all that well. I felt like the organization was losing confidence in me too, and with good reason. I pitched my worst game of the year on Tuesday, April 28th against the Tuscon Toros. I pitched the second game of a doubleheader. We won the first when Pat Jacquez tossed a two-hitter to lead us to a 2-1 win. Ed Honeywell was not too kind to me in the Tacoma Tribune the next day: *"The inept effort was Darcy Fast's in the nightcap—the Lacey lefty surrendered five hits along with three walks in one and two-thirds innings, yielding all the enemy runs in the process, and the Toros hung on to register a 6-4 conquest."* I walked three in that short stint, and even though we failed to pull off a double play when our second baseman made another error behind me, I had to admit that I wasn't getting the job done like I had the previous year. It was very frustrating.

I didn't pitch much better during my next outing on May 2nd against the Phoenix Giants. I gave up three earned runs in 2 innings and part of the third, walked one, and didn't strike out a single batter. I was 0-4 with a 5.96 ERA, the worst on the team, and I had managed to throw just 19.2 innings over those four starts. I was just searching at that point to find my old form and thought I'd better figure the problem out soon. That must have been the last straw for the Cubs. On May 8th, my baseball world was flipped on its ear.

Comedy of Errors

In 1968, Denny McClain of the Detroit Tigers won 31 games with a 1.96 ERA and won the MVP award in the American League. Bob Gibson had a 1.12 ERA in 1968 and Carl Yastrzemski of the Boston Red Sox that same year won the American League batting title with a .301 batting average. It was the "year of the pitcher"—scoring was down and pitchers were putting up unbelievable numbers. The owners figured fans wanted to see more scoring and decided to lower the pitching mound to make things easier for hitters. Of course, that meant they were making it harder for pitchers, like me. Even though my shoulder didn't start hurting until 1970, I still wonder if the league's decision to lower the mound contributed to my shoulder woes —I'd never had trouble before, and pitching off the lowered mound meant changing my arm angle quite a bit. The top of the rubber, beginning in 1969, was no higher than ten inches above home plate. From 1903 through 1968, the limit was around 15 inches, although it was a very nebulous limit and some of the mounds were as high as 20 inches. The Los Angeles Dodgers, known for their pitching, had the highest in the majors. It felt like you were pitching off a hill—like you were just naturally falling off the dirt—when you could rock off a fifteen or twenty inch pitcher's mound. In 1969, it became harder to follow through after delivering a pitch. I wasn't the only one who had arm trouble, either.

Umpires also started narrowing the strike zone during that time, and teams started bringing their fences in five or so feet. The message was loud and clear: let the home run parade begin! I'm sure all of this has contributed to the explosion of great power hitters over the last twenty years. Steroids explain part of it, but even steroids wouldn't have helped someone hit a Bob Gibson fastball when he was tossing from that higher mound.

The league expanded after the 1968 season as well, and added four teams: the San Diego Padres and Montreal Expos in the National League, and the Kansas City Royals and Seattle Pilots in the American League. In October of that year, when they held the expansion draft, I heard that San Diego was very interested in picking me up, but the Cubs decided to protect me. Teams could protect 15 players; when one player was drafted, the team could protect three more. There were rumors flying around that I might get traded to the Padres, after all, once the 1969 season got rolling. I remember Fred Martin came out to me during spring training and told me that San Diego had their eye on me, but that the Cubs "froze" me—that felt good, because it meant they still believed in me. At the time, however, I actually thought it might be good for my career to go to another team. I figured the Padres would give me a chance to be a starting pitcher right away. I also relished the idea of breaking in with a much younger team, as it would be easier to make the cut when there were no talents like Holtzman or Jenkins around. All of this was in the back of my mind all through the spring training of 1970.

It wasn't a total shock when I got the news. Whitey Lockman, the Tacoma manager, came to my motel room one morning around 8 o'clock.

"You got a minute, Darcy?" he said. I was a little surprised to see him, since he didn't usually make house calls. I figured I was in for a pep talk.

"Sure thing, Skip."

"You've been traded to the San Diego Padres. You're going to report to the Salt Lake City Triple-A team." He shook my hand. *"We'll miss you in the Cub organization, but this is a great opportunity for you."*

That day I realized baseball was a business. He handed me a plane ticket, and I was on my way to Salt Lake City. It all happened that fast. I took a newspaper with me onto the plane and I found it a bit unsettling to read the following: "Right-hander Rich James will rejoin the Tacoma Cubs. Bobby Adams, president of the T-Cubs, announced Friday that left-hander Darcy Fast had been traded to the Salt Lake City Padres for James in a straight player swap." I learned later that the Padres had actually thrown a second player into the deal, but that didn't matter—being traded still stung a bit. On the one hand, it felt like the Cubs had given up on me, but on the other, it felt good to be wanted by San Diego. I thought about all the guys I'd played with in Tacoma, like Jim Colborn, Roe Skidmore, and Terry Hughes; I also thought about how I wouldn't see them much anymore. Then again, I also thought I would have a real chance to pitch for the Padres. They won only 52 games in 1969, and the fact that they traded for me meant they believed in what I could do. They definitely needed me more than the Cubs.

As it turned out, the Padres were still in the process of putting a decent team together, and many of the guys on the AAA squad wouldn't have even been in Double-A on the rosters of more established teams. The Padres still didn't have enough guys to field four minor league teams. The Pacific Coast league was known as the most competitive league in Triple-A, so I knew we were in for some rough times. We became a kind of "Bad News Bears" that year—we blundered and stumbled our way through the season.

The manager for the Salt Lake team was Don Zimmer, a hot-tempered manager (even back then). The team was bad, of course, and he didn't like to lose. Don Zimmer had made the major leagues with the Dodgers in 1954 as a second baseman and played part time over four seasons before having his best year in 1958, batting .262. Zim was not a great hitter, but he was known as a terrific competitor. In fact, he nearly died after getting hit with a pitch in the minor leagues in 1953, but that didn't stop him from coming back to the game he loved. He stayed with the Dodgers when they moved to Los Angeles in 1958, but then played for the Cubs, and later with that awful Mets expansion team in 1962. He played with the Reds, and again briefly with the Dodgers, before finishing his career with the Washington Senators. In his twelve seasons he batted .235, drove in 352 runs, and stole 45 bases. He saw plenty of losing—perhaps accounting in part for his ill-temper—but he also played in the World Series with the Dodgers in 1955 and 1959. Zim was a very good fielder—besides second, he played third, short and outfield in his career. He even caught a bit when he was with the Senators his last year. He just liked to compete.

Zimmer went on to a long coaching career, as most baseball fans know. He managed the Padres for a few years before being fired, then coached third base for the Boston Red Sox. He was promoted to manager by the Sox in 1976 when the team let Darrell Johnson go midway through the season—he led them to 90-plus wins in each his three full seasons. Unfortunately, he is also known for leading the team that coughed up a huge lead to the Yankees in 1978. The Sox had a ten game advantage in August (sound familiar?) but stumbled and actually fell behind the Yankees. The Sox, after rebuilding a four game lead, got beaten by the Yankees in four straight games in September in what is still called "The Boston Massacre." There are additional similarities to the Cubs' infamous 1969 collapse: the manager (in this case, Zimmer) played the catcher almost every day. Hall of Famer Carlton Fisk caught 154 out of 162 games. Also, Zimmer stuck with a beat up player for too long—he kept running third baseman Butch Hobson out there, but Hobson had chips in his elbow and couldn't throw. His errors piled up until Zim finally had to bench him. When he did, the team rattled off eight straight wins. The team ended up losing to the Yankees in a one-game playoff when light-hitting Bucky Dent lofted a home run over the Green Monster in Fenway. Fans have never forgiven old Don for that collapse, but it's easy to forget that the 1978 Red Sox won 99 games! Zimmer went on to manage the Rangers and, of course, the Cubs, winning manager of the year in 1989. I find it interesting that he managed two of the hardest luck teams of the past 100 years. Zimmer also had three stints as a coach with the Yankees, and even another one with the Red Sox, under manager Butch Hobson in 1992.

Many people also remember the infamous brawl in the 2003 American League Championship Series when Zimmer charged out of the dugout and tried to tackle pitcher Pedro Martinez. Martinez tossed the then 72-year-old Zimmer to the ground, to the horror of everyone watching. When I saw that I thought, *"Ole Zim hasn't changed a lick,"* because I had a few run-ins with him myself when he was managing the Salt Lake squad back in 1970. I basically got along with him, because we both wanted to win ball games, and we were both frustrated with the way things were going. However, when I came over from Tacoma, they expected me to pitch better than I did. I actually had a decent ERA, but I just wasn't getting wins. In one game where I wasn't pitching well, Zimmer came out and lifted me from the game. I was disgusted with myself and fired my glove into the dugout. Zimmer thought I was showing him up; he thought I was upset that he'd taken me out of the game. Actually, I was just disgusted with myself. He didn't know that, though, and came tearing after me. I was halfway up the runway to the clubhouse when suddenly I felt someone jump on my back—it was him! I'd never been jumped by a manager before, of course. He yelled and screamed and told me not to show him up, that it was unacceptable. I tried to fight him off and tell him I was just mad at myself. Finally, the other players came and tore him off me and that was the end of it. Zim didn't even say anything afterwards. The next day when I came to the ballpark Buzzy Bavasi's son, Peter Bavasi, was there and looking for me. Buzzy was the GM of the Padres, but Peter really didn't know too much about the game at the time—he'd had little contact with it. Regardless, he insisted on having a meeting with me and Zimmer. By that time, Zimmer had forgotten all about what had happened, because that was just the way he was: he needed to blow off steam and once he did, he was fine. Peter tried to arbitrate. He sat us down and tried to have us talk about our feelings and emotions. It was comical. It was like he was trying to apply something he'd learned in a Human Resources class. Zim and I started laughing. Finally, Zim couldn't take it anymore, and asked Peter to leave his office.

The losing continued for our squad, though in hindsight, it was inevitable. Some of the players were Triple-A caliber, but many weren't even Double-A. Sometimes you just had to laugh to keep from crying. In my second start with the Padres, we faced the Tacoma Cubs, of all teams. I was fired up to beat them, because I'd just been traded and I wanted to show them that I could still pitch. Things were going well. I had command of my fastball and I was striking guys out again. We took a 2-1 lead into the seventh when it happened: our rookie right fielder, Jim Williams, misplayed a routine fly ball. He tried to get under it, but I guess it just kept moving on him—he made a last second dive, but it bounded by him. In the eighth, it was déjà vu all over again. The Cubs had a man on first when another Tacoma hitter lofted a routine fly to shallow right. Poor Jim had even less luck with that one, as it bounced by him and allowed the base runner to score all the way from first. It was a shame because we'd taken the lead with 2 of our own in the top half of the seventh, using a leadoff walk by Walk Hriniak (who later became a famed hitting guru), a double by center fielder Jerry Morales, and later, a beautiful squeeze bunt. We ended up losing 3-2 and my hard luck continued. I'd pitched eight innings, gave up seven hits, struck out five, and only had one base on ball, but my record dropped to an abysmal 0-6. I was more upset to lose that one, too, because it was against my former team. Dave Lemons, a good friend, was the opposing pitcher; I'd felt I'd thrown better than him that day. A beat writer came up to me after the game and said he couldn't believe the way the season had gone. He called me *"Unlucky Fast."*

When we landed in Tacoma after that game, JoAnn met us at the airport. She'd decided not to go to Salt Lake in the first place because we didn't think I'd be there that long. When Zim saw her he said, *"What can we do to get that black cat off Darcy's back?"*

It started to turn into a crazy season. In one game, I was pitching against the Phoenix Giants when a wicked one-hopper came ripping back through the box from Jimmy Ray Hart and caught me square on the butt. I grabbed the ball, flipped it to first and then doubled over in pain, waiting for the cavalry to arrive. Soon our trainer, Bobby Fleischer, raced out of the dugout. He looked me over, scratched his head and said, "How's your arm, Darcy?" I didn't have the heart to tell him it wasn't my arm that was burning like someone had just kicked it!

Ray Herbat, writing for the Salt Lake City Bee, even penned an article about our team entitled "Laughing It Up... Life With Loser Can Be Hilarious." There was a grainy photo of Don Zimmer with the piece—he's attempting to smile, but looks instead like someone who just found out his dog has gone missing. From the piece:

> *"Then there was the time when Larry Stahl was batting a cool .406 but was not playing this night because a lefthander was pitching for the opposition. Stahl also had a slightly pulled muscle in this leg. So Manager Don Zimmer gave him a brief rest. Along about the eight inning, the fans sitting along the third base line near the coach's box started to get on Zimmer pretty good."*
>
> *"How come, you dummy, Stahl's not in the lineup?" one of them yelled at Zimmer. Zimmer, who usually ignores the taunts, this time shot back over his shoulder with: "I can't use him." "Why not," the fan asked. "Oh, he was up in the mountains today skiing and broke his leg," Zimmer lied. The fan gasped, then wanted to know if Zimmer fined Stahl for such a stupid stunt. "Naw," Zim said with a straight face. "What are you gonna do?"*

At the time Herbat wrote the article, on July 18th, 1970, we were in last place, 28-and-a-half games out of first. He concluded by saying, *"Such is life with a loser."*

Towards the end of the season, I was called up by the Padres, but at almost the exact same time I also received notification from my National Guard unit in Salem that the Veteran's of Foreign Wars convention would be held in Portland, Oregon. I had to report within two hours. Part of me couldn't believe it, but I didn't have a choice—I had to report. I was placed on "ready alert" during the convention. Our unit would be activated along with others if there was trouble with Vietnam War protesters. It was almost like what happened with the Iraq War in 2007. Folks were really concerned in Portland that there were going to be a lot of problems.

The Padres were not pleased with this news, and they didn't want to believe me. They thought I just didn't want to report. Can you imagine not wanting to report to a Major League baseball team? They thought I didn't want to report beause they were just a new team.

"No." I said, *"I can't report. My company commander has told me that I have got to be on ready alert. I have to be able to report to them within two hours."*

I had to call the San Diego Padres and explain to them what was going on again. They didn't accept my explanation, and I had to get my company commander to write them a letter. But they *still* didn't accept it. They stopped payment on my contract, and that made me wonder what San Diego really thought of me. If they could just stop payment on my contract, what was my future going to be like with them? It's hard to believe a guy would not want to go to the major leagues, but that's what they thought. It wasn't true, of course.

I couldn't wait to get back to the majors. Baseball players didn't have agents in those days, and in spite of my phone calls, explanations, and a letter stating my military obligation, the Padres stopped payment on my contract for failure to report.

Back then, there were no agents representing 20 and 21-year-old kids and none of us had experience working with baseball management—that's just the way baseball was. It was such a privilege to play that you didn't dare go into the manager's office and say, "I'd like to have a raise!" I felt abandoned by the Padres and major league baseball.

In January of 1971, I received a phone call from the Padres' new General Manager, Eddie Leischman, who wanted to discuss my status with the team. He was not aware of the circumstances that prevented me from joining the big league squad the year before and agreed to pay my remaining 1970 salary and send me a new contract for 1971. I didn't hear from him and the Padres again until Preston Gomez called me from Yuma, Arizona the week that pitchers and catchers reported early for spring training. He wanted to know why I wasn't there with the other players and I told him that I had not heard back from Eddie Leischman about my contract. He said Mr. Leischman had died suddenly and unexpectedly, and that he would get the matter resolved immediately with the front office. I was stunned and felt bad about Mr. Leischman's passing. A few days later, I had a new contract, a check for the remainder of my salary, and an airline ticket for spring training in Yuma. I then had to call Preston back and explain that because of my uncertainty as a player with the Padres, I had made financial and business commitments that would prevent me from playing that season. I had decided to wait on the season and consider what the future had in store.

I greatly missed playing during the 1971 season and though I kept busy, I knew I could still eventually return to baseball. After the season was over, I received a phone call from George Freese, the Chicago Cub scout who signed me, and who was my first professional manger. He said he was now working with the Padres and wanted to make an appointment to see me in Lacey to convince me to return to the game. He told me that there was still a good chance I could pitch for the Padres the following season, and he assured me that he had spoken with Preston Gomez; I would be given every opportunity to become a starting pitcher or used in long relief.

I finally decided that what George said that day made sense, and after thinking it over for a time, I called him back and told him I would sign for the 1972 season. He was extremely pleased with my decision and told me a new contract would be sent out shortly. I didn't tell him how much I was struggling to make this decision, though. I'd done nothing my whole life but strive to make it in the big leagues – that's why I'd been so dumbfounded by the Padres. Of course I wanted to play ball! Who could doubt that? But now, with time away from the game, I could sense God guiding me in a different direction and I wondered if I should consider retirement. Most ballplayers come to a point in their careers when their bodies give out and they have no choice but to hang 'em up. But I did have a choice. I was entering my prime and was just beginning to understand how to really succeed as a pitcher. I had years ahead of me, in fact. And if I decided to hang up my cleats, I knew very few people inside or outside of baseball would understand. *What was he thinking*, I imagined people saying. *He had his dream and he just let it go*. I also didn't want to let down the people who had coached and supported me. More importantly, I didn't want to let myself down. I had worked hard to succeed as a ballplayer and I didn't want to quit until I had given it my best shot. It's difficult to give up your life's dream, after all, but I began to see that I needed to listen carefully to God.

As the start of spring training in 1972 drew closer, I became more uncertain: should I play, or should I allow God to guide me into something else? It didn't help to read the article, "New Look for Padres" in The Sun Newspaper, where Preston Gomez said that *"the return of Darcy Fast could help considerably his '72 pitching staff."* Then one afternoon, when I was at my lowest, I pulled out a box of all my old baseball memorabilia and began taking the pieces out one by one. I was feeling pretty frustrated and unsure about the direction of my life and somehow I thought going through the box – seeing pictures of Hank Aaron, Roberto Clemente, Willie Mays, Ernie Banks and other famous ballplayers that a Cubs' photographer had given me – would give me an answer. There were old, beat up baseball gloves and hats that I'd worn in Little League, all crumpled up in there. I pressed one of the gloves to my face and breathed in the sweet, leather scent of baseball. It was wonderful and brought back a flood of memories. I also discovered a horseshoe that a grounds-keeper at Cheney Stadium had given me for good luck. I browsed through the Cubs playbook from my first pro season. I pulled out the weighted ball I used to strengthen my arm and started flexing again, as if I was about to step onto the field. I pulled a couple of baseballs out of the box and turned them over in my hand, getting the feel for them. There was one I used to throw my first pitch against the Atlanta Braves – I flashed back to the way the sun felt on my face that day, the way my heart nearly broke free of my body. I pulled out the ball I threw to get the final out when I set the Pacific Coast League strike-out record – there was a tiny scuff mark where the bat had contacted the ball. I lost track of time sitting there pouring over all that old stuff. The nostalgia, I guess, was pretty irresistible. I sat there for hours and would probably have stayed longer, but my reverie was disrupted. My wife JoAnn walked into the room with our baby boy—Christian. I looked into my wife's face and could tell immediately that she was flat-out worried. That snapped the spell and got me thinking. The items in that box had, until that moment, represented the most important thing in my life. But baseball was only a game. And maybe I'd been blind all these years. Sure, I loved the game and always would, but it suddenly wasn't as important as my family. And my destiny. In a few weeks I was supposed to report with the other pitchers and catchers for spring training, but my heart wasn't in it anymore. It was time to give up this kid's game and accept whatever God had planned for my life. I threw all that old stuff back into the box. I remember very clearly reaching up and putting it back on the shelf in our closet that day. It stayed there a long time before I ever opened it again.

Chapter 10

Extra Innings

One Chair

Luciano Pavarotti, the great tenor who passed away in September, 2007, often told the story of how he made the decision to commit himself to becoming a singer. At a young age, his father introduced him to singing, and he took to it with great skill and enthusiasm. Later on he found himself studying with a professional tenor and at the same time preparing to be a school teacher. When he graduated, he faced a dilemma: which profession to embrace? When he asked his father about which course to take, his father responded: *"If you try to sit on two chairs, you will fall between them. For life, you must choose one chair."*

I found myself in this awkward position for many years – I continued my business and teaching pursuits and involved myself in the ministry on the side. I knew that God was looking for a full-time commitment from me, but I just wasn't ready. I served in the church and helped with my father's radio program, *Wondrous Grace*, but I was doing all of these things on my terms. I couldn't commit to sitting in one chair.

I remember when I finally said yes to God's calling. During our church's Family Camp one summer, I was attending the evening service when Pastor Gerald Marvel was preaching and I heard God speaking to me in that still, quiet voice. Throughout the service I felt as if God were saying, *"Darcy, I've been calling you into the ministry for some time, but you always have an excuse. I'm calling you one more time."* I began to see that He'd been calling me since high school, but I'd thought that if he would just let me become a major league ballplayer, I'd give him all the glory. Now that I was out of baseball, I had no more excuses. I'd come to the point where I either needed to embrace His call or turn my back on Him.

During your average baseball game, when the starting pitcher begins to tire, the pitching coach makes a "call" from the dugout to the bullpen to get a relief pitcher into the game. I learned to listen attentively for that call throughout my brief stint in the majors. We all answer many different types of calls in life. Some are important, while others are just minor irritants. But when it's God's call, we had better listen. In the Bible, Samuel, under the direction of God, chose David to be the King of Israel. David knew that God had placed a call upon his life. God places his call on all our lives at one time or another.

Could I have helped the 1969 Cubs hold off the Mets? I'll never really know. It's water under the bridge now. I chose to write my story in part to ask myself that question, but also to inspire people who might be out there wondering what their mission in life should be. I was one of the youngest players ever to voluntarily retire from major league baseball. I don't know if that's something to be proud of or not, but it's something that I decided to do because I knew back then that I needed to accomplish something bigger with my life. That "something" started at a young age and built throughout my life. The older I got, the more it built. I enjoyed being in business and teaching school, but I still wasn't satisfied—something was missing. I wasn't helping people. When I looked back at the people who'd meant the most to me in my life, I realized they were all people who took the time to care about me. They were willing to sacrifice some part of themselves to help me learn, or to make me a better, stronger person. My dad was the perfect model. There were many things he could have done with his life, but his love and passion was the ministry. He wanted to help people grow spiritually. Growing up, we didn't have all the things a lot of kids had, but we had a fabulously strong family. My mom and dad really loved and believed in what they were doing, and I saw the personal satisfaction that they got out of it. After struggling for many years, I finally began to figure out that I wanted to do what my father had always done: help people.

In my sophomore year of high school, I drove with my family from Washington to Anderson, Indiana: the headquarters of the

Church of God. Located there is Anderson University, Anderson Theological Seminary, and the General Offices of our church. Those offices today help to oversee over 3000 congregations throughout the world, and every year about 25,000 people gather in the summer for the International Convention of the Church of God. My parents knew how serious I was about athletics back then, and they didn't want to do anything to discourage me. My dad bought me a book called <u>The Bobby Richardson Story</u> to show me that a person could be an athlete and a Christian man. We drove for hours on hot, dusty roads in a Pontiac, and I devoured that book. Bobby was a tremendous leader. He was an all-star second baseman for the New York Yankees and a tremendous Christian.

The book really inspired me. I thought, "There's a guy who can play professional baseball and be a Christian and have a great influence on people's lives." I was still consumed by baseball at the time, but the book affected me and continues to dwell in my heart. We had a great time as we drove all the way out to Indiana and back. You can be a Christian and play baseball, I thought. You can play baseball and do something meaningful with your life afterwards.

Other people, like the great Dodgers' pitcher of the late forties and fifties, Carl Erskine, also inspired me. He was born in Anderson, Indiana on December 13, 1926. He played baseball very early in his life, learning very quickly how to throw fastballs and curves. He also had part of his career interrupted by World War II, as many guys did in the forties. The war ended when he was very young, and he quickly made it to the majors. Erskine got to play with legends such as Gil Hodges, Jackie Robinson, Pee Wee Reese, Roy Campanella, Duke Snider, and Carl Furillo. Fans nicknamed him "Oisk," which was their New York way of saying the first syllable of his last name. He went 21-10 as a relief pitcher before becoming a starter in 1951. He pitched in five World Series, and finally won in 1955 against the New York Yankees. There were only seven no-hitters thrown in the Fifties, and he threw two of them. When the Dodgers moved to California, Erskine didn't like the travel and being away from his family, and so, after about a year and a half, he retired. He was only 32. I always remembered that. When he retired, he went on to run a successful business. He also coached baseball for twelve years at Anderson University, winning four championships.

In my childhood, I ate, drank and breathed baseball, and I already knew how great Erksine had been. He also made no bones about his Christian faith, and this inspired me to be strong about my faith. I also was amazed to see that he'd stepped away from baseball at a young age, and I ended up following in his footsteps (though I retired much younger than he did). I didn't get to meet Carl when my family visited Anderson University, but I finally did run into him just a few years ago when the All-Star Game was played in Seattle—I was invited to go to a Major League Alumni Association meeting of former major league players, and he was there. I told him that I became a minister after my baseball career, and that he'd been an inspiration to me. He said, *"I've always been thankful for my baseball career because it has given me many opportunities to influence people's lives for Jesus Christ."*

If I'd told anybody during my baseball career that I was thinking about the ministry, I would have had to be accountable for it, and early on, I didn't want that. I thought I would have to give up too much to be a minister. I wanted to be successful. I wanted to make good money. I wanted to become a great pitcher or first baseman. I knew that if I went into the ministry, I wouldn't have fame, money, notoriety, and all the things that went with being a ballplayer. What I didn't realize then was that I had to give up my own desires to find something better. Sitting there that day, listening to Pastor Marvel, hearing the words of God, I knew. I finally understood: there was no more sitting between the chairs for me. That evening, after the service, I made the decision to commit myself totally to God's will.

From the moment I fully committed myself to the ministry, God moved in my life. He began to give me opportunities to share my story and to speak about the message of saving grace through Jesus Christ. People that I respected and admired began to confirm the call of God upon my life. Even when I told JoAnn about my decision to follow God's call, she said she already knew it. He had prepared her as well. God doesn't call us and keep it a secret from others. Responding to His call, I attended Bible College and Seminary, though I've come to realize that my greatest preparation for the ministry was given to me by my parents. I will always be grateful for their Godly example and teaching.

I had many great experiences in professional baseball, but my satisfaction and joy has been far greater in the ministry as I've helped people find a personal relationship with Jesus Christ and grow spiritually. I believe many people endure a similar struggle in their lives. They wrestle with their dreams and they're not sure of God's purpose for their lives. Sometimes people are too focused on what they might lose by following God's calling, such as fame, money, glory. Instead, we should take a careful look at everything we gain by following His will: love, respect, purpose.

Of course, you don't have to become a minister to find God's purpose for your life. You can go into any profession: baseball player, writer, doctor or teacher. For me, it just so happened to be the ministry. In fact, baseball, in just the short time I played, opened up many doors and opportunities for me, allowing me to share and talk with people about their lives. When I retired from baseball, I was only 24. Nobody fired me. I went on to something that I thought was much better for my life and I've never regretted it. I know now, as I did then, that I found God's purpose for my life.

Decisions

Life is full of tough decisions. Everyone wants to make the right ones, but it's hard to know what those are. Since retiring from baseball, the majority of my life has been devoted to leading a dynamic group of Christian people at Centralia Community Church of God. As their senior pastor, I am repeatedly asked about decisions people must make. Often, they want to know how to find what God's will for their lives.

Some decisions are relatively easy to make and some are very difficult. My decision to leave a professional baseball career was not an easy decision. It came over a long period of time as I struggled to choose between baseball and a higher calling. But we all have to make decisions: what college should I attend, what job should I pursue, who should I marry? Most of the time we have enough information to guide us. Maybe not enough to guarantee the outcome, but enough to help us make a good choice. At times we ask ourselves, "How do I know I'm hearing from God and doing His will? What does he want me to do?"

Recently, while staying in New York at the Sheraton Hotel and Towers, I was startled out of bed at 2:30 a.m. by hotel fire alarms and a message over the loud speaker: *"There is a fire, evacuate your room immediately."* I threw on my clothes and quickly looked out my window to see New York City Fire Department personnel with fire trucks and emergency vehicles surrounding the hotel. It was a frightening experience. I ran into the hallway to find other dazed people coming out of their rooms. I told them they could follow me as we made our way down nine stories of stairs. When we finally got to the lobby there were hundreds of other people milling around, sleepy-eyed and scared. The hotel manager told us to wait for further instructions. But when the loud speaker crackled back to life to give us more information, the message was muffled and distorted. You could sense the frustration throughout the lobby. I thought to myself, I'm so glad that God speaks to us in discernible thoughts.

God's guidance is constant and consistent. He never gets out ahead of us and He makes it possible for us to understand Him as He is giving us directions. Proverbs 3:5-6 has been a favorite scripture of mine since childhood. It was given to me by my parents and it has helped me at every stage of my life. It says, *"Trust in the Lord with all your heart, and lean not on your own understanding. In all your ways acknowledge Him and He will direct your paths."*

What an awesome promise from the Lord. It's a clear promise of guidance and protection, and something we need everyday in our lives—guidance and wisdom in what to say, how to react to what others say to us, and what to do in all kinds of situations. What do we do when we come to a fork in the road and we have to make a major decision? Those are the times we need to know how to get guidance from God. How do we receive guidance for our lives? We have clear teaching in Scripture and the guiding presence of the Holy Spirit. The Holy Spirit is our helper and gives us strength and power to live the Christian life. The Bible is our guidebook, as it is written by one who has journeyed before us. I have also found that guidance comes from within the circumstances of our lives.

One spring evening, JoAnn and I were watching our son play one of his first baseball games. Shortly after the game started, I overheard a lady say to the man standing next to her, *"Excuse me, you're in what type of business?"*

"I'm in professional baseball," he said. She looked puzzled and he told her he was a scout for the Chicago Cubs. He said he was here

visiting with his son's family while on business. I decided to turn around to meet him and asked him if he had heard of Darcy Fast.

"Yes," he said, *"I'm responsible for him playing in the Major Leagues with the Chicago Cubs."*

I told him I was Darcy Fast and I shook his hand. He was H.D. "Rube" Wilson, a special assignment scout, and I was just as surprised to see him as he was to see me. He had scouted me when I was playing in the minor leagues, and based upon his report to the Chicago Cubs, I was set to pitch in the majors. He was in the Pacific Northwest to scout a Seattle Mariner's pitcher that the Cubs were interested in obtaining. Throughout the game that evening, we talked about our lives. We talked about some players we knew and the pros and cons of playing professional baseball. He then said something I will never forget.

"Do you see that man who is coaching your boy's team? That's my son, and because of my 30-year career in baseball, I never saw him grow up. I have a lot of catching up to do."

I knew what he meant. When you're playing baseball, you're away from your family for long periods of time. As we were driving home after the game, I asked JoAnn, *"What was the likelihood that I would meet Rube Wilson on a grade school baseball field and find out about the decisions that affected my baseball career?"* Was this just a chance meeting or was there some higher purpose to it? I believe God allowed me to meet Rube so that He could confirm for me that entering the ministry was the right choice for my life. I had never met this man before. God uses the circumstances of our lives to give us guidance and direction.

I became a major league baseball player, but I gave it up. I went into business, but gave that up. I had to do those things to find my purpose. Now, looking back, it all makes sense—my choices led me down an inevitable path because I trusted in God. I sometimes think of life as a melody playing on one of those old LP record albums: there's a single groove, with bumps and valleys; you can't change what was playing before or know what's coming next. You can just shoulder responsibility for your actions and believe. I believe I was destined to become a minister. It's easy to see that now, but as I lived it, I often felt confused and lost. Finding my purpose, my groove, in life—something almost every human being struggles with—was a difficult journey, but it was also rewarding and enlightening.

When people ask me how to find God's purpose for their life, I tell them it's not something I can answer for them. But I tell them that if they commit their life to Jesus Christ, if they work hard at what they love, if they learn to care for themselves and others, then they won't have to worry: the answer will find them. Like a symphony played on a record player, eventually the important motif will come around. You just have to be awake to hear it.

Printed in the United States
95724LV00003B/125/A